Little
flowers
in silk and organza ribbon

"The earth laughs in flowers."
Ralph Waldo Emerson

Little flowers

in silk and organza ribbon

by Di van Niekerk and Marina Zherdeva

SEARCH PRESS

This book is
dedicated to all the
embroiderers, wherever
they are in the world.

Thank you for your support
and encouragement.
We hope you will enjoy
the projects.

Patterns for Double Roses and Blue Violets, Strawberry Blossoms, Ring of Daisies and Wild Roses and Pink Blossoms are © 2014 Sonie Ames Designs, Utah, USA. Pattern for Rose Wreath © 2014 Di van Niekerk and Verde, Cape Town, South Africa. All the other patterns in this book are © 2014 Marina Zherdeva, Moscow, Russia.

First published in Great Britain in 2014
Search Press Limited
Wellwood, North Farm Road, Tunbridge Wells, Kent, TN2 3DR

Originally published in South Africa in 2014 by Metz Press,
1 Cameronians Ave, Welgemoed 7530, South Africa

Copyright © Metz Press 2014

Text copyright © Di van Niekerk and Marina Zherdeva

Photographs and illustrations copyright © Di van Niekerk, Marina Zherdeva and Metz Press

Publisher   Wilsia Metz
Design and layout   Claudine Henchie
Proofreader   Hazel Blomkamp, Thea Grobbelaar
Illustrations   Wendy Britnell
Photographers   Marina Zherdeva & Di van Niekerk
Reproduction   Color/Fuzion
Print production   Andrew de Kock
Printed and bound by Tien Wah Press, Singapore

ISBN 978-1-78221-104-4

47

55

Contents

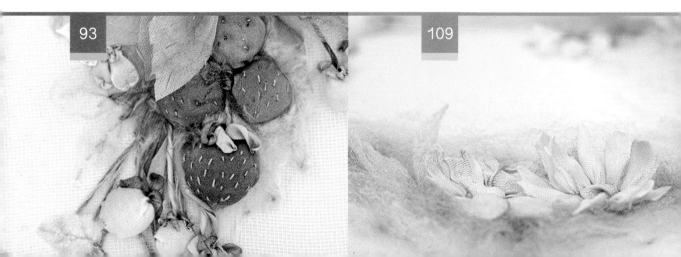

93

109

65

75

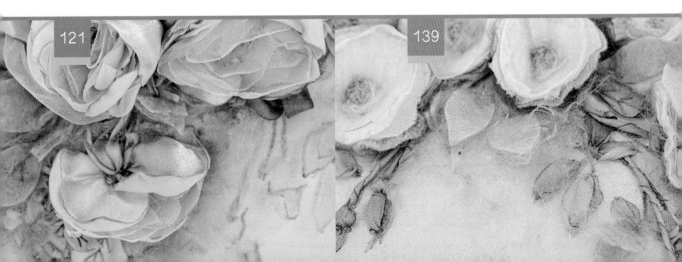

121

139

Preface

In 2012 I was fortunate enough to travel from Cape Town, in South Africa, to faraway Russia. In Moscow I viewed Marina Zherdeva's remarkable creations and it made perfect sense that we write a book together to introduce Marina's incredible talent to all embroiderers, no matter where they are in this world. My dream was to create a book that would combine the style and techniques from two different, but equally creative countries, on two diverse continents, and to share it with the world of embroidery. This book is the culmination of that dream and we hope that it will bring you many hours of joy – the same joy that Marina and I experienced whilst creating these designs for you. Enjoy yourself and happy stitching!

Di van Niekerk

Silk ribbon embroidery appeared in Russia just a few years ago and this wonderful needlecraft enchants more and more Russian women with its beauty and magnificence. Meeting Di van Niekerk in the fall of 2012 was a remarkable event in my life and it's a great pleasure to be a part of this unique international embroidery project – writing a book as a co-author with the most creative and talented embroiderer, a world famous and reputable author, a charming lady and my dear friend. Presenting our projects we would like to show you how easy and rewarding silk ribbon embroidery really is; how simple it is to combine different techniques in one flower project with glorious results. You will soon learn how good this kind of embroidery is for the soul ... try it and soon you will love this glamorous needlework forever!

Marina Zherdeva

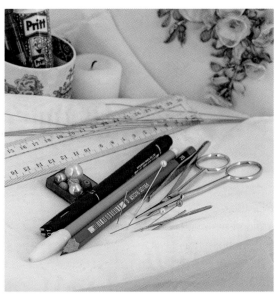

Getting started

Tracing designs onto fabric

Hint: Patterns are included with every project. Use a black pen with a fine point to trace the patterns onto a sheet of tracing paper or a sheet of white paper. This way, you won't be tracing directly from the book which could leave unsightly pen marks. You could also make a photocopy on a copier: in colour for the Rose Wreath and in black and white for the other projects.

Depending on the project, you will use a water-soluble pen (lines disappear when drops of water are placed on them – we will explain how in the projects) or a sharp 2B pencil – every project will guide you. Place the fabric on top of the tracing paper and pin or tape in place. Trace the design as neatly as possible. Work on a light box (or glass table with a light underneath it) to make the tracing more visible if using a darker fabric. When tracing with a pencil, keep sharpening it to ensure fine lines. The pencil does not wash out and the fine lines will be covered with stitches. Draw softly and use a ruler for the straight lines. Draw 2 mm ($\frac{1}{16}$ inch) inside the leaves and flowers on the design. This prevents pencil lines from showing once embroidered. You could also mark the position of small petals and flowers with little dots.

Fabric and backing fabric

Background fabric

A luxurious, soft, medium-weight fabric with a relatively high thread count is a good choice for this kind of embroidery. Select from white to ivory to the very palest shades for silk fabric. Choose a white or natural colour for linen and cotton. The fabric should complement the design, be strong enough to hold the stitches, and the pattern should be visible through the fabric for tracing.

Choose Dupion silk, pure linen, silk-satin and silky voile, cotton and linen blends or pure cotton fabric. It's up to you. Choose the fabric and shade that you like best. **Note:** If using a soft, sheer fabric like silk organza, voile or chiffon, place it over a similar shade of silk-satin fabric which will act as a support. A backing layer will be added too. See Backing fabric in the next section.

Hint: When using Dupion silk, it is best to wet the fabric before you start and to iron it dry with an iron set on steam and an appropriate temperature. This wet processing prevents shrinkage and visible traces of water on the surface when removing outlines from water-soluble marking pens. Silk shrinks by 5–10%, so make sure the initial size of the fabric is big enough to fit in the 25 cm hoop, plus allow for the shrinkage. Remember that silk is a delicate natural fibre and the fabric requires careful treatment. Please try to avoid creasing; minor bruising of the fabric is eliminated by ironing with steam.

Note: The background fabric should be large enough to fit easily in your hoop. For a 25 cm (10 inch) hoop, you could use a 35 cm (14 inch) background block. For Dupion silk use a slightly larger block to allow for shrinkage.

Backing fabric

Note: This is an optional step and it is possible not to use a backing layer at all. Before you start to embroider, an additional layer of fabric could be added behind your background fabric/embroidery panel. The backing fabric acts as a stabiliser and it will be easier to end off threads and ribbons at the back of your work. A soft white or cream to pale grey organza or chiffon is a good choice. You could also use soft muslin or any silky fabric. Ensure that the backing fabric is the same size as the background block.

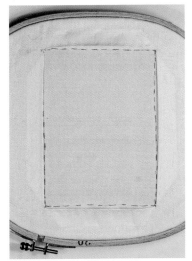

cut-out, equal in size to your embroidery design shape. Place your embroidery panel on a flat surface, lay the dust cover fabric on top, and cut a window the size of your design. With running stitch, tack the two layers together along the "window's" edge. Another option is to place the dust cover with the "window" on top of the layers (without basting or tacking) before inserting them into the hoop. See Rose Wreath on page 78 for more information and pictures.

Hint: Work with clean hands. Clean hands are vital when working with silk ribbons. Your completed embroidery will look perfect if the fabric and ribbons are absolutely clean, without traces of dirt, paint or cream. Keep your embroidery clean; avoid even touching the embroidered elements.

Hoops

Hoops are essential when working with fabric and ribbons as they keep a drum-tight tension and allow you to regulate it during work. Use a round or a square wooden hoop. A quilting hoop (which is a bit thicker than the embroidery hoop) is a good choice if you have one. The thicker hoop will hold the fabric layers and the stitches more securely. To make the tension tighter and to prevent the fabric from sliding, wrap the inner circle with strips of cotton or linen fabric and secure with sewing thread.

Allow for a relatively large border of the fabric around the embroidered area (10 or 15 cm/4 or 6 inches) when choosing a hoop from your collection. Choose a hoop that is larger than the design you will be embroidering to keep the completed stitches intact. A 25 cm (10 inch) hoop is a good choice. For smaller stumpwork shapes, use a 10 cm (4 inch) hoop or a 15 cm (6 inch) hoop.

Keeping your work clean

To keep your work clean, use an additional layer of cotton or thin linen to protect the space around your embroidery area whilst working. The dust cover layer should be the same size as your embroidery panel, but it has a "window"

Stretching fabrics in a hoop

Lay the inner circle of the hoop on a flat surface and, with backing fabric at the bottom, place all the layers on top of the ring. Place the outer ring over the inner one and tighten it halfway. Stretch the fabrics taut as a drum. Pull gently when you stretch, smoothing out every layer. Don't distort the fabric – a gentle, even tension is required. Check that every layer, especially the backing fabric, is crease free and tighten the wing nut. Roll up the corners of the fabric and pin or tack them out of the way.

Hint: Remember to tighten the layers in the hoop, every now and then, so that the background does not pucker; pull all the layers gently along the edge and tighten the wing nut. ·

Material requirements

What ribbons and threads do I use?

We have listed the requirements with each project. As a rule, most of these items are easily obtainable from your local needlecraft store. If you are having trouble locating any of the requirements, please feel free to contact us at di@dicraft.com or marina.zherdeva@gmail.com and we will happily assist you with your query.

About the ribbons and threads

Pure silk ribbons were used for the designs in this book. Choose silk taffeta ribbons for their crisp, smooth, lustrous fibre and the flowers and leaves will appear almost lifelike, with petals as soft as they are in nature. Try to use the hand-painted ribbons with a variation in colour. Light and dark areas on the ribbon will help to form the shadows and the highlights. We used my own range of ribbons in this book and the codes are listed with each project in case you need them. These ribbons are available from needlecraft stores worldwide and you will find the details on our website www.dicraft.com under the "my stockists" button.

Note: The ribbon looks quite coarse in the photographs, which are of such high quality that the camera has picked up the fibres in the silk. The ribbon is actually as smooth as silk.

Organza ribbon was also used for some of the projects. This ribbon is available from stockists worldwide. Please feel free to use ribbons of your own choice. As long as the ribbon is a fine, crisp, smooth taffeta silk and the organza not too rough a weave, the designs will turn out well.

The threads we have used are mainly DMC (or Maxi Mouline equivalent) and Rajmahal Art Silk. But do feel free to use whatever brand you prefer and try to pick a similar colour to match the design.

Hints on using thread:
Separate the strands and work with only one strand, unless suggested otherwise.

To start: make a knot at the long end or use a waste knot which will be cut away afterwards as follows: start with a waste knot 7.5 cm (3 inches) away from the shape. Once the shape is complete, cut the knot and pull the thread to the back. Insert the thread into a needle and end off by running it under the stitches at the back.

To end off: gently run needle and thread under stitches at the back or make small stitches into the backing fabric (if you have used backing). Be careful not to pull ribbon stitches out of shape.

Allow your needle and thread to hang off the back of your work for the thread to unwind as soon as it starts to twist or knot. When working with two strands of thread, separate one strand at a time then place them together to thread the needle. This way the threads are not twisted around each other, allowing for a smooth finish.

About the needles

It is essential to use the correct size needle for threads and ribbons, and the sizes are listed with each project. The needle must make a large enough hole in the fabric for the ribbon to pass through without being snagged or damaged. This way, the ribbon spreads to form a soft, open stitch instead of being scrunched up when pulled through a hole that is too small. The eye of the needle should also be long enough for the ribbon to fit into.

The needles to use for this kind of embroidery are:

Crewel/embroidery: a sharp, fine needle with a long, large eye. Use size 9 for the DMC and metallic threads and size 10 for one strand of the Rajmahal Art Silk.

Quilting/betweens: short, sharp needle with a large eye. Very easy to thread. Use size 9 or 10 for one strand of thread if you find the crewel needles are too difficult to thread.

Chenille: a thick needle with a sharp point and a long eye.

For the following widths, use the sizes listed below.
- 32 mm ribbon – size 13 chenille or tapestry
- 13 mm ribbon – size 16 chenille
- 7 mm ribbon – size 18 chenille
- 4 mm ribbon – size 20 or 22 chenille
- 2 mm ribbon – size 22 or 24 chenille
- Metallic, DMC plus other threads and large beads – size 28 chenille is useful or use crewel/embroidery needle as listed above.

Tapestry: same as a chenille needle but with a blunt tip. Useful for shaping stitches and to use as a supporting structure when forming loose, raised stitches. Insert needle under the stitch as it is formed. A size 13 tapestry needle is ideal for this.

Wool and silk fibres

For some projects in this book, silk and wool fibres were introduced to show you how to build softly shaded backgrounds. This option could be used with any of the projects and we have shown you how to do this in the last four projects.

Small wisps of wool or silk fibre, gently teased apart and placed behind the flowers and underneath the leaves, add an interesting dimension and the colourful feathery texture creates an almost ethereal quality. You could also use the fibre to fill shapes as shown in the Strawberry Blossoms and Poppies projects. The fibre from a silk rod is gorgeous, lustrous and a wonderful filler; it adds dimension and saves you time too. Tear off small pieces of the rod and place in the centre of the flower. We will show you how in the relevant projects.

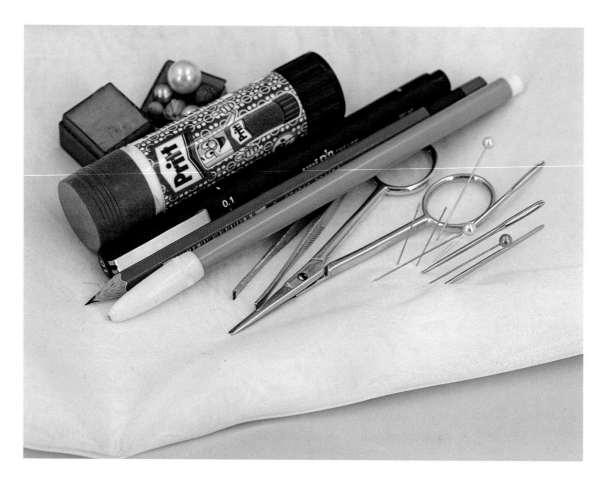

What else do I need?

☑ **Scissors:** small, sharp embroidery scissors are a must. They are a very helpful tool to cut threads and ribbons and snip holes in the fabric when needed. Never use these scissors to cut paper or wire, keep them safe so that the ends remain sharp; also prevent them from falling. Dressmakers' scissors will be useful to cut fabric for projects.

☑ **Needle grabber:** a thin piece of rubber, which will help to pull the needle with ribbon through the fabric.

☑ **Thimble:** leather or other thimble – use one if you prefer.

☑ **Pins:** pins with colourful plastic heads are useful tools to temporarily fix elements in place until you secure them with a thread.

☑ **Wire:** aluminium wire for beadwork 0.3 mm wide is perfect for stems and stumpwork. Green no. 26 cake-decorating wire is also good for flower stems.

☑ **Wire-cutters or nail clippers:** to trim wire. Or use old scissors instead.

☑ **Sewing thread:** simple, fine sewing threads that match the colour of your fabric, leaves and petals are useful when securing and shaping stitches. They play a supporting role and should not be visible on the embroidery.

☑ **A glue stick:** similar to what the kids use for school projects.

☑ **Clear liquid glue:** is clear andtransparent when dry. It must dry quickly. This glue is applied in very thin lines or dots; excess is removed with a paper napkin. This glue is used to strengthen the edges and prevent them from fraying.

☑ **Glitter glue:** is useful for the edge of the butterfly wings.

- ☑ **Water-soluble fabric and anti-fray agent:** both are available from machine embroidery shops and needlecraft stores. Use a clear liquid anti-fray agent and test that it dries clear. Water-soluble fabric looks like a fine plastic film and it dissolves in water. You could make your own glue by dissolving water-soluble fabric in water. See page 28 for more information.
- ☑ **Paper tray:** plastic transparent horizontal paper tray (or a couple of them) placed one on top of another is convenient for keeping everything you need ready at hand for each project. Not a must, but is very helpful.
- ☑ **Tablecloth:** white paper tablecloth (medium size) organises your working space and helps to keep embroidered pieces, threads and ribbons clean. Place the tablecloth over the desk – being white it reflects the falling light, which is always friendly for eyes. When the process is interrupted, just collect all items into a tray, fold the tablecloth in half and fix the edges with paper clips. When you start the process, simply unfold the tablecloth – everything will be ready at hand for clean and comfortable embroidery.
- ☑ **Pens and pencils:** you will need a water-soluble marker, sharp 2B pencil and black pigment ink pen (water and fade proof) with a fine tip.
- ☑ **Cosmetic sticks or Q-tips/ear buds:** they are useful to erase water-soluble pen marks and for reshaping petals and leaves.
- ☑ **Floss box:** plastic compartmentalised box to keep threads in – not a must, but helpful.
- ☑ **Daylight or good lighting** and a comfortable chair.
- ☑ **A ruler:** mm/inch

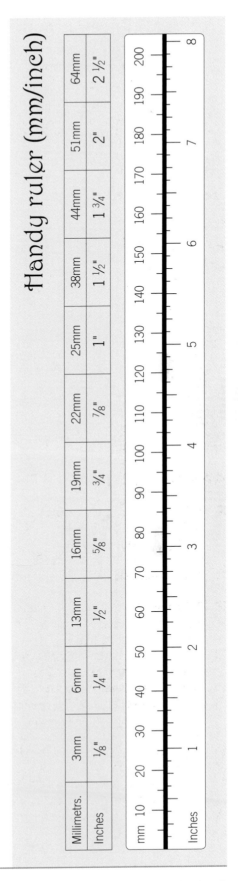

Handy ruler (mm/inch)

Millimetrs.	3mm	6mm	13mm	16mm	19mm	22mm	25mm	38mm	44mm	51mm	64mm
Inches	1/8"	1/4"	1/2"	5/8"	3/4"	7/8"	1"	1 1/2"	1 3/4"	2"	2 1/2"

Ribbon techniques

Threading ribbon

Thread needle and pierce the end that has just been threaded; pull the long tail to tighten the knot. Refer to Threading ribbon in the Stitch gallery on page 160.

To start the stitch
When starting with ribbon you have several choices:

a. Leave a small tail at the back and when you make your first or your second stitch, pierce the tail to secure it onto the fabric.
b. Or for the wider ribbons, secure tail with embroidery thread and stitches. This is a most effective method.
c. Or knot the 2 and 4 mm ribbons as you would a thread if the texture of the design is busy enough to hide the bulkiness of the knot.
d. Or make a looped knot: fold tail of the ribbon onto itself and pierce the fold with needle. Pull needle and ribbon through the fold to form a loop-like knot.

To end off

Leave 1 cm (⅜ inch) tail at the back; secure with small stitches. Trim tails for ease of stitching. Always secure the tails behind the elements of embroidery (petals, leaves or stems) and try to make it a habit. Some day when you would like to embroider on organza, your work will be accurate and perfect. This habit is very useful when you embroider curtains or lampshades.

Note: For starting and ending threads, see About the ribbons and threads on pages 13 to 14.

Working with ribbon

How long must the ribbon be?

Use short 20 to 30 cm (8 to 12 inch) lengths of ribbon, especially with the 4 and 7 mm ribbons. The wider (13 mm and wider) ribbons should only go through the fabric two or three times to prevent fraying. For the 2 mm ribbons, a longer length of 30 to 45 cm (12 to 18 inches) works well as this ribbon does not fray as quickly as the wider ribbons do.

A note from Marina: To make silk ribbons shine even brighter and make them even softer, iron with steam before embroidery – the result will exceed all your expectations. What I value most in ribbon embroidery in comparison with thread embroidery is the lifelike volume and shape – our ribbon embroidery looks like a charming bas-relief sculpture. Working with a gentle tension allows the ribbon to spread to its full width on the fabric before the next stitch is formed. Do not make the stitches too tight, as the ribbon will fold and the beautiful silk texture and volume will be lost.

Dark colours can be seen through pale background fabric when not covered by other stitches or elements and it is best to end off and start again if there is a large gap between the stitches. I always cut 13 mm and wider ribbon on the back after each stitch and secure the tails. This helps me to form each petal individually and prevents the previous stitches from losing shape if the needle hits them accidentally.

When making a new stitch, try to avoid piercing the embroidered ribbon on the back. Move the ribbons aside with your needle and come up through the fabric when possible. Pushing the ribbon through the fabric is much easier than through the silk ribbon (or several layers of ribbon) and this does not harm the previous stitches.

For wide ribbons (13 mm and wider) I use two needles to make a petal or leaf: the first needle makes the tail and starts the stitch (working from right side of fabric) and the second one is used to end off a stitch. Thus the ribbon does not go through the fabric and it retains its smoothness and shine. Use the needle grabber to help pull the needle with ribbon through the fabric.

Storing ribbon

Ironed ribbons always give a perfect result. To keep them smooth and glossy for a short period, gently roll up and store in a box. To prevent them from creasing and tangling while working on the project, use cardboard rolls from paper towels or toilet rolls. Paper rolls can be cut along the edge to secure the ribbon tails. The tail is fixed to the roll with a pin. Plastic or paper floss cards are also suitable but folded ribbon should be ironed before embroidery.

Making holes in your fabric

To make a stitch with wider 7 mm and 13 mm ribbons, it is a good idea to make a hole in your fabric before you make the stitch. This way, the ribbon will not be damaged and it's easier to pull the ribbon through the fabric. Use an awl or stiletto, or a size 16 chenille needle; pull needle all the way through the fabric. Then insert needle and ribbon through the hole. The ribbon opens up once the stitch is formed and covers the hole. When you use a stab stitch to secure the ribbon, pull the ribbon into place gently as you form the stitch, to neaten the base of the petal or leaf.

Working with wide ribbon

Silk ribbon is a very delicate fabric and when wide ribbon goes through the fabric, it creases no matter the size of the hole it goes through. Once embroidered it is impossible to iron the ribbon. To make sure the ribbon retains its flat intact surface, try to avoid drawing wide (25 mm and wider) ribbons through the fabric at all. With 13 mm ribbon: no more than two or three times at the most. To make a shape from a wide ribbon (25 mm and wider), cut a piece the desired length of the leaf or petal and add on two tails (twice x 2.5 cm or 1 inch). Form a double ribbon stitch on both ends of the ribbon (see page 23) and take each tail to the back individually, working from the right side of the fabric. Use a needle grabber where needed.

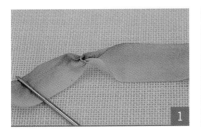

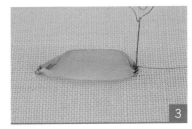

Securing and shaping stitches

To shape a stitch: Silk ribbon is very sculptural and pliable and will retain any form you wish to create with it. To secure the shape of the leaf or petal, use a sewing thread or one strand of embroidery thread of a matching colour and make a tiny stitch as follows: come up with needle and thread, catch the very edge of the silk ribbon and insert the needle into the same hole in the fabric. This stitch is almost invisible and the secured petals and leaves will maintain the form that you have created.

To secure a stitch: Use one strand of matching thread and tiny stab stitches (short, straight stitches) to secure the tip and the base of the stitch. This way, the ribbon will not pull out of shape when you make the adjoining stitch.

Working with two needles

You will use one needle with ribbon to make the petal or leaf and another needle with thread to secure it. Always have one needle on the top of your work. If both needles are at the back of your work, they will become entangled.

Ribbon stitch

To make a regular ribbon stitch, insert the needle in the middle of the ribbon's width. Use a gentle tension and flatten the ribbon before making the stitch by running the side of the needle under the ribbon to iron out the creases.

Insert a cotton ear bud (or similar object) under the ribbon to push the ribbon outwards before forming the stitch. This helps to form a soft, rounded stitch.

To make a ribbon stitch that curls to the right, insert the needle on the right-hand edge.

To make a ribbon stitch that curls to the left, insert the needle on the left-hand edge.

To make a twisted ribbon stitch for an interesting leaf or petal, twist the ribbon before piercing it.

To make a cylindrical shape, twist the ribbon several times before piercing it.

Do you see how one stitch becomes a different shape, depending on where you insert the needle, and whether you twist it or not?

- -

Hint: Use a cotton ear bud or a tapestry needle to gently lift the stitch, if necessary.

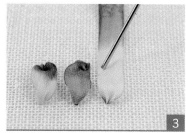

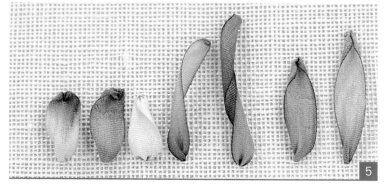

Double ribbon stitch

Double ribbon stitch is a two-step method using the ribbon stitch principle to make pointed leaves and petals (see page 159). Fix the ribbon's short tail on the back. Prepare the ribbon as if you were making a ribbon stitch. Do not take the ribbon through the fabric. Slightly lift the ribbon and pierce it with the needle. Gently pull the needle and the ribbon through to make a ribbon stitch.

Take the needle through the ribbon again. Now insert the needle into the fabric and gently pull the ribbon to the back until the sharp end touches the fabric. Cut the ribbon at the back and secure the tail with thread and tiny stitches.

- -

Hint: For extra sharp points, repeat the process and point the needle back into the same hole.

- -

More interesting techniques

Long twisted stems

Twisting ribbon: Stems made with twisted straight and twisted ribbon stitch are almost lifelike in appearance and surprisingly easy to make. Come up from the back and twirl the needle and ribbon to form a tight coil before taking the needle to the back again at tip of the stem. Use a gentle tension and allow the ribbon to unwind at the back before coming up to form the next stem. This will prevent loops from forming at the back of your work. See Twisted straight and Twisted ribbon stitch in the Stitch gallery on page 159 and 160.

Sometimes the beginning of the ribbon is not ideally cylindrical. In this case, gently pull the ribbon on the back until you are happy with the shape. Use matching thread and tiny stab stitches, and secure the beginning and the end of the stem and any loose sections of the twisted stem. These stitches are only necessary where the stem is a bit wobbly and where it needs to have more of a curve. Work between the twirls so the stitches are almost invisible.

Hints: If you twist the ribbon clockwise, the stem will bend clockwise; twist it anti-clockwise and the stem will bend in the opposite direction. When the fabric is light in colour or translucent, threads and ribbon could show through from the back. Take care not to jump too far to make the next stem or stitch. Rather end off and start again.

Stems from wire

To add dimension and structure to a flower, wire can be used to form free-standing stems that are raised from the surface of the design. For each stem you will need: 10 to 13 cm (4 to 5 inches) of 0.3 mm beading wire, 20 cm (8 inches) of green 2 mm silk ribbon (or you could use stranded cotton) and a glue stick used for school projects.

Cut a length of wire: 10 to 13 cm (4 to 5 inches) with old scissors or wire-cutters.

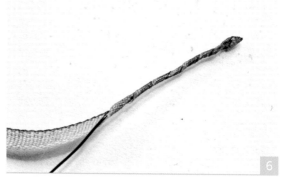

Make a small (5 mm or ³⁄₁₆ inch) loop on one end of the wire.

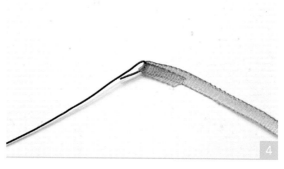

Glue the ribbon (or cotton) along its full length.

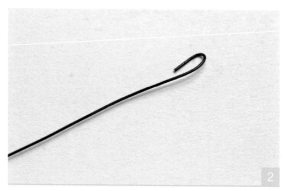

Press one tail of the ribbon to the surface of the glue and pull it through until the end. Glue must cover only one side of the ribbon or cotton.
Fix the ribbon or cotton in the loop and press down to glue in place.

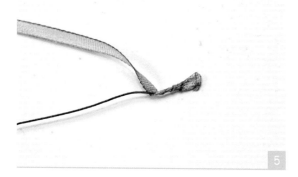

Fold the ribbon or cotton around the wire, with the glued surface facing the wire, and working quickly, wrap the wire.

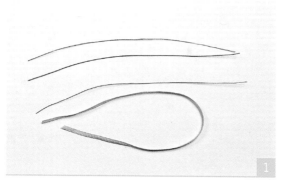

Make sure the edges of the twisted ribbon or cotton fit neatly alongside each other – the wire should not be visible.

As the glue dries very quickly, before reaching the other end, you may need to add some more glue on the free ribbon or cotton to make sure it won't unfold. Wrap to cover the wire completely.

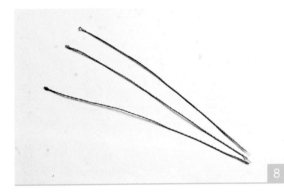

Fix the tail with glue, allow the stem to dry.

Hint: Fold the looped end over again to make a small loop that will fit snugly in the flower a little later.

Free-standing ribbon tails

Easy-to-make, free-standing ribbon tails are ideal when you need to add extra volume. Ribbon is secured along the one end – the end that is lying against the fabric – while the other end is loose or free-standing. An example of where narrow, free-standing tails of ribbon were used most effectively is in the Rose Wreath under the section: Rose bud with open sepals on page 82. For the narrow tails, glue can be applied afterwards to protect the ends.

There are many variations when making free-standing ribbon tails. Some flowers, like the poppies and the roses, are wonderfully voluminous and are made of wide ribbon. For these wide petals, it is best to avoid a bulk of

ribbons on the reverse and we will show you how to shape the ribbon and how to make the tail narrow at the back while the petal on the right side remains wide and spectacular. For the wide petals, make sure that the ribbon is protected from fraying by using a water-soluble processed ribbon (which is preferable) or applying some glue along the edges. We will show you how.

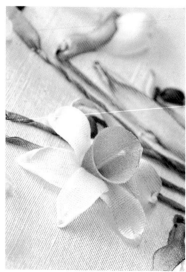

Make your own anti-fray liquid glue with water-soluble fabric

Water-soluble fabric is very useful when you need to strengthen the ribbon and prevent it from fraying when making separate 3D elements. Take a piece of a water-soluble fabric 5 x 5 cm (2 x 2 inches), cut it into small pieces, place into a small jam bottle and cover with 2 teaspoons of very hot water. Stir while it dissolves to make a concentrated solution. Place a piece of ribbon in this solution and soak it for a minute or two, remove and allow to dry slightly. Iron the ribbon. Single treatment does not guarantee that the ribbon will not fray when you actively disturb the edges, but it will help for when you accidentally touch the ribbon with a thread or a finger. To make sure the edges of the cut ribbon remain intact it is best to repeat the above process a few times. Or you could use liquid transparent glue (see more about glue on page 16).

Making loose leaves and petals

Loose petals and leaves are easy to make and add a lovely dimension to your design. Some shapes are made from organza fabric and ribbon, others from silk ribbon, silk paper and rods. We will show you how with the strawberries and the roses in the chapters that follow.

- -

Hints: When cutting out organza shapes, work on a white tablecloth or sheet of white paper. The outlines on the organza will be more visible.

- -

The same applies when tracing directly onto the ribbon: use a sheet of white paper underneath the tracing for a better outline.

Apply an anti-fray liquid on the edge of the shape to prevent fraying. The liquid will spread onto the entire shape.

- -

Hint: Use a thick sheet of white paper so that the anti-fray agent does not make a mess on your table. Use a dry towel or face cloth to gently pat the shape dry. See Make your own anti-fray liquid glue on page 28.

- -

Place shapes on a towel, in groups, alongside each other. Cut small squares of paper and mark the groups according to their symbol or number: A, B C... allow time to dry.

The petals are now ready to be curled or to be placed onto your design. Handle with care to prevent fraying of the edges. We will show you how in the chapters that follow.

Sealing the edges of petals or leaves

The edges of the loose petals or leaves can be sealed with heat so that they curl up to form lifelike shapes, as for the double roses on page 121 and the wild roses on page 139. **Note:** these petals are made from a synthetic satin and organza fabric.

Method: Trace the petal and do not apply anti-fray. Singe the edges on a candle flame. Hold the petal or leaf with tweezers and have a bowl of water nearby in which to insert the shape if it catches alight. Hold the shape 5 cm or 2 inches away from flame as the heat will melt the shape too much if too close to the flame.

Hint: The curved edge can only be achieved with synthetic fabrics – pure silk ribbon will not curl up. However, this is a good method to use to seal the edges of dark shades of silk. Silk will have a burnt edge which is visible on the pale shades and the use of an anti-fray agent is then advised.

Making 3D ribbon flowers

Three-dimensional flowers are so lifelike and such fun to make! Daisies, poppies and poppy seeds have been used successfully in the designs in this book and we will show you how.

3D chamomiles

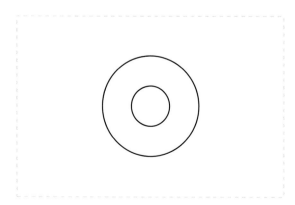

3D chamomile template

Note: See page 26 for making stems from wire.

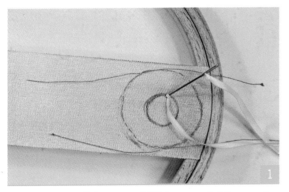

Fix a 32 mm ribbon no. 132 (or any light green) in a 10 to 15 cm (4 to 6 inch) hoop.

Use a water-soluble pen to draw a circle, as shown above. The inner circle has a diameter of 10 mm (just over ⅜ inch) and the outer, larger circle is 24 mm (almost an inch).

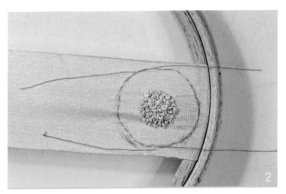

With 2 mm ribbon no. 95, fill the small circle with French knots, wrapping the ribbon once around the needle.

Make two layers to add volume. Using the strand of green thread, make short running stitches along the outer circle as shown.

Hint: Stitch two semicircles instead of one circle and leave long tails of thread to gather them easily when completing the flower.

Make the white petals, embroider loop stitches with 4 mm ribbon no. 103.

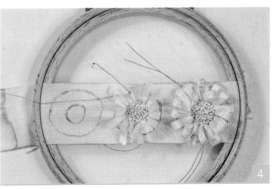

To flatten the loops: use a small amount of glue on the tip of the needle and spread evenly on the inside of the ribbon loop. Lightly press between your fingertips, aligning the edges neatly. Allow the glue to dry.

Hint: While the glue dries, make a stem as described on page 26.

Cut the embroidered flower out of the ribbon, adding a 5 to 6 mm (almost ¼ inch) seam on the outside of the large circle.

Pull the thread tails, gather edges and make a kind of pouch; fill it with a small piece of toy filling or woolly fibre.

Fold the seam inside the pouch and insert the looped end of the wire stem inside. Tie the thread tails together tightly. Do not cut the ends, just conceal them.

Use one of the thread tails to make several stitches through to tighten the pouch and secure the filling and the wire stem. Now trim the tails of the thread to complete the flower.

The three-dimensional chamomile is ready!

See Chamomiles on page 65.

Shape the stem according to the design and secure the flower with tiny stitches.

- -

Hint: Insert the wire stem under the embroidered elements for a natural effect.

- -

3D poppies

Make a collection of poppy flowers in different stages of growth for your design!

Hint: For ribbons and materials, see Poppies on page 55.

For how to make the wire stems, see page 26.

3D poppy template

Making the petals

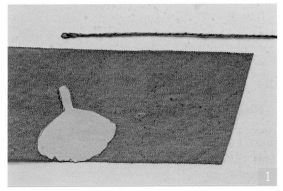

With a water-soluble pen, trace the poppy template onto the ribbon with tiny dots.

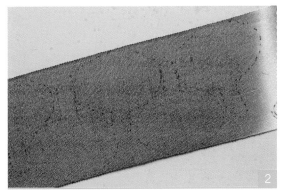

Here we used 32 mm silk no. 141.
Pay attention to the variation of colour on the ribbon and choose the best option.

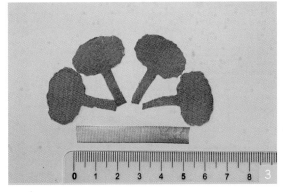

Cut out the petals. Leave tails of 1.5 to 2 cm (about ¾ inch) long.

Carefully apply transparent glue to the edges of the petals. Allow the petals to dry. Remove the excess glue with a paper napkin or your fingertip.

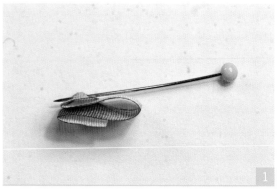

Make the pistil

Cut 5 cm (2 inches) of the green 7 mm ribbon no. 36 and fold it as shown. Length of the ready-made pistil is 13 to 15 mm (½ to ⅝ inch).

Stitch the edges together with tiny stitches and one strand of matching thread.

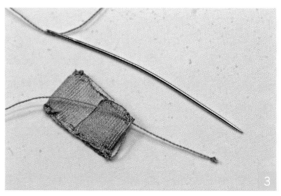

To turn the ribbon inside out, pierce one of the upper corners.

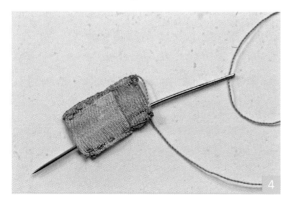

Accurately insert the needle between the layers of ribbon and gently pull the thread.

After the pistil is turned right side out (as shown), cut the thread. Carefully push out the corners with the sharp end of your scissors or a similar object.

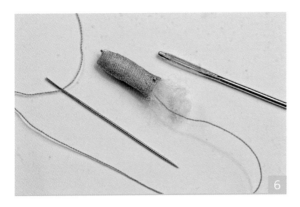

Fill two-thirds of the pistil with toy filling or wisps of woolly fibre – see Wool and silk fibres on page 14. Use the sharp end of your scissors or blunt end of a needle.

On the pistil, embroider stigma with pale yellow thread and little back stitches. Use Rajmahal Art Silk no. 44 (one thread) and a fine needle so as not to damage the shape.

Embroider stamens with looped back stitch and Rajmahal thread no. 29, making loops along the edge. Leave a 2 mm (1/16 inch) seam – work a little away from the edge so as not to damage it. Leave the loops uncut.

Make the poppy
Insert the tail of the petal into a large chenille needle and take it through the pistil, piercing the pistil close to the edge. Petals should cover the stamens' loops.

Hide the tail inside the pistil.

Repeat for the other petals.

Hide the remaining petal tails inside the pistil.

The poppy flower – reverse view.

Poppy flower – front view.

When all tails are hidden, insert the prepared wire stem inside the pistil. Close the edge with tiny stitches and matching thread. Cut the thread.

Spread the loops of the stamens.

Cut the loops. Cut the thread at desired length. The poppy flower is ready!

3D poppy seed pod

See page 26 for making stems from wire. For this stem, you will need 13 cm (5 inches) of wire and 17.5 cm (7 inches) of the 2 mm ribbon no. 25.

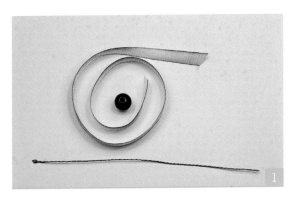

To make a seed pod you will need:

- 1 x 10 mm (just over ⅜ inch) bead with a wide hole
- 30 cm (12 inches) 7 mm ribbon no. 36
- wired stem

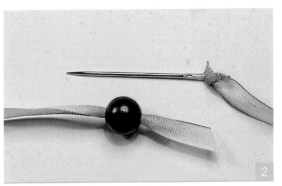

With a small chenille needle, take ribbon through the hole of the bead three times, trying not to pierce the ribbon inside. Spread the ribbon so that every next turn it overlaps the previous one by one-third.

Pull the ribbon firmly to fix the tail.

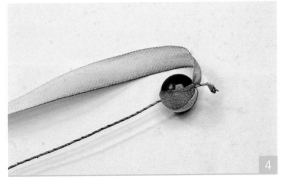

Insert the wired stem and fold the upper end as shown.

Continue to wind the ribbon, overlapping turns by one-third of the ribbon width. Gently pull the stem to hide its end inside the bead.

A total of six or seven turns are fine. Cut off the ribbon.

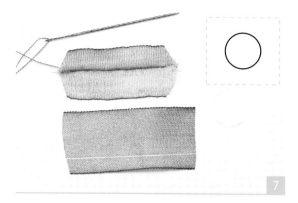

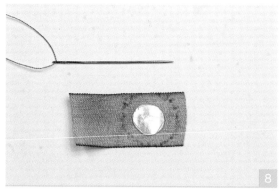

Take a small piece of bottle plastic and cut out a disc with diameter of 8 mm (⁵⁄₁₆ inch). You may use either strips of 7 mm ribbon no. 36, stitched together as shown, or 3 cm (1¼ inch) of 13 mm ribbon no. 25.

Mark a circle with a diameter of 12 mm (½ inch) around the plastic disc.

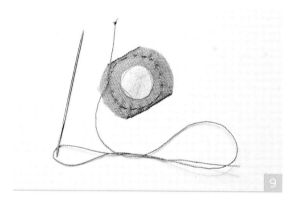

Outline with small running stitches and cut out as shown, leaving a tiny 2 mm (¹⁄₁₆ inch) seam.

Pull the thread to gather and enclose the disc.

The top of the pod is ready.

Attach the top to the pod. Wrap the junction with thread two or three times. Secure with small stitches; cut the thread.

Make segments with one strand of Rajmahal thread no. 311.

The poppy seed pod is ready!

3D poppy bud

See page 26 for how to make stem from wire.

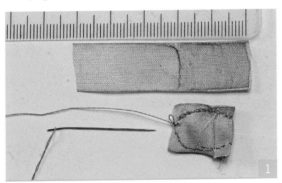

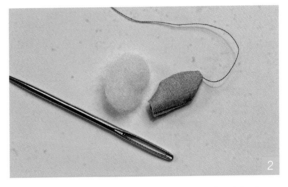

You will need 5 cm (2 inches) of 13 mm ribbon no. 32 or join two pieces of 2.5 cm (1 inch) 7 mm ribbon no. 36 – your choice. With one strand of green thread, make an oval shape as shown. Secure a short thread on the top to turn the bud out (as you did for the pistil on page 34).

Turn the bud right side out and, with the blunt end of a large needle, fill it with toy filling or woolly fibre. See About the wool and silk fibres on page 14. Do not cut the thread.

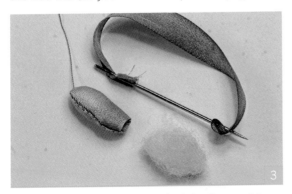

Take 5 to 6 cm (2 to 2¼ inch) of the 7 mm ribbon no. 141 and make a looped knot at one end. Pierce the folded end: pull needle through ribbon to make a knot. Insert needle through the green bud so that it emerges at the tip of the bud.

Start with a knot inside the green bud and make a zigzag line of tiny running stitches as shown. Use a matching thread.

Pierce the ribbon through the side seam.

Gather the thread; spread the ribbon. Secure the ribbon with the thread and hide the tail. Cut the red thread.

Insert the wire stem into the bud. Secure the bud and the stem with the green thread. Close and neaten with tiny stitches and cut the thread.

The blossoming bud is ready!

3D spent poppy

See page 26 for making stems from wire.

To make the pistil take 3 cm (1¼ inch) of 7 mm ribbon no. 36; fold it as shown and sew the side edges with short running stitches or back stitches.

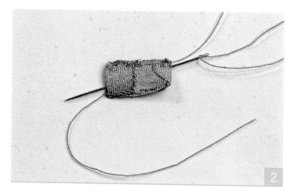

Turn the pistil right side out as shown on page 34.

Fill it with toy filling or woolly fibre with the blunt end of a large needle or the points of your small scissors.

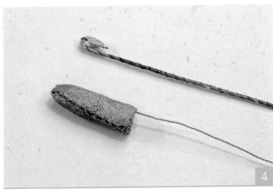

Insert the wire stem into the shape.

Secure the edge and the stem; cut the thread.

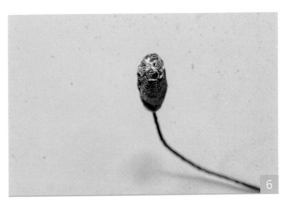

Make the stigma with small back stitches. Use one strand of Rajmahal no. 44 and a chenille needle size 28 or embroidery size 10 for very fine work.

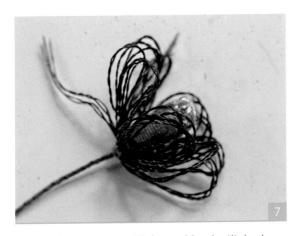

Embroider stamens with looped back stitch along the edge. Use two strands of Rajmahal no. 29 thread. Leave 2 mm (1/16 inch) between the edge and the seam.

Cut the loops. Sometimes the thread is crumpled. To straighten it, just wet it and allow it to dry.

Make the stamens of desired length to suit your design and your taste.

Pistil, stigma and stamen.

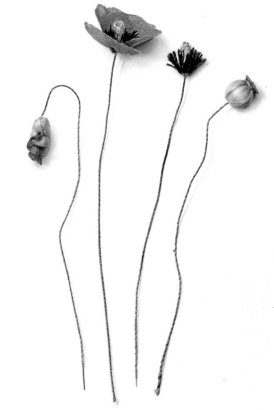

A spent poppy flower is ready!

The four stages of 3-D poppies.

Little creatures

Small creatures add life to the design and always attract some attention! Though they take some time, they are easy to make or embroider and will decorate your work perfectly. We'll make some of them – butterflies, bees and even a little spider.

Spider

A metallic thread (Madeira silver) is used as a spider web thread.

Tiny straight stitches are the legs.

Use a French knot made with Rajmahal no. 29 or a tiny (15°) black bead for the body.

So quaint!

Wings can be embroidered with Madeira metallic thread to add a little sparkle.

This little bee was embroidered for the Chamomile design on page 65. With Rajmahal no. 29 and tiny straight stitches, fill in the black stripes as shown above.

With two strands of Rajmahal no. 94 or 144, make the yellow stripes in straight stitch. Make the legs and antennae in no. 29; use straight or back stitch. The little wings are made with silver metallic thread and straight stitch.

Alternatively, to make a fluffy bee, use the same black no. 29 (two strands) and yellow no. 144 (two strands), and make Turkey stitch or looped back stitches. Cut the loops and fluff with the sharp point of your needle. Trim until you are happy with the texture.

Repeat for the little bee on the left-hand side of the design. Use one strand of the black as before and change the yellow to two strands of no. 94 thread. Add the wings in silver metallic thread and use straight stitches as shown.

3D silk ribbon butterflies are easy to make and almost lifelike in appearance. This butterfly can be used with the Narcissus design (see page 47).

It's important that the ribbon wings do not fray and it is a good idea to use a water-soluble processed ribbon (see Make your own anti-fray liquid glue on page 28 and you can apply clear liquid glue along the edges).

Note: Use 32 mm silk ribbon for the wings. Orange is no. 51 and blue is no. 88.

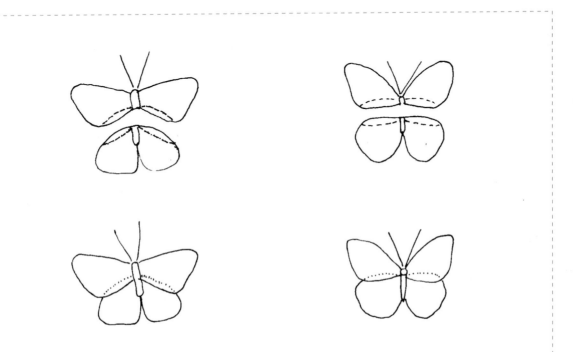

Utilise the shading on the ribbon for a lifelike effect. Trace part of the wings onto a pale section of ribbon and the other part onto a darker section, depending on the ribbon. Gently cut out the wings with very sharp embroidery scissors.

Place wings so that they overlap slightly. Apply a tiny drop of glue on the overlapping area between the wings and apply pressure to glue in place.

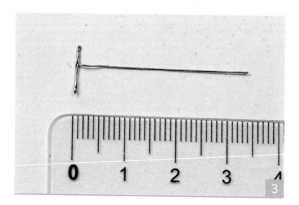

Use 0.3 mm beading wire or fine stumpwork wire and make a wire holder for the body of the butterfly. The ruler size above shows 3.5 cm (1⁶⁄₁₆ inch).

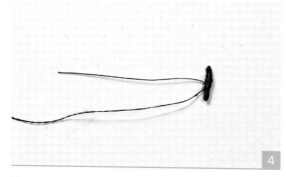

Use a 40 cm (16 inch) length of Rajmahal no. 129 thread (one strand) to wrap the wire. Pull the thread through a glue stick to make sure it does not unwind. Make the antennae as shown.

Make a hole in the middle of the overlapped area with a needle of similar size and insert the wire holder into it. Apply a tiny drop of glue and stick the butterfly's body to the wings.

To make the antennae, use one strand of no. 29 Rajmahal thread, apply glue (glue stick or transparent liquid) to the thread and allow to dry. Insert the thread into a needle and take it through the wrapped threads of the body. Trim to the desired length and gently re-shape with your fingertips.

For natural-looking ends, use dark brown fabric paint mixed with a thickener (Marabu or Javana) and very carefully paint the antennae and around the outer edge of the wings. Allow to dry.

Make a hole in the background fabric where you want to place the butterfly. Use a chenille needle. Insert the wire to the back and position the butterfly as you would like. Bend the wire at the back to flatten it and secure with tiny stitches.

Narcissus

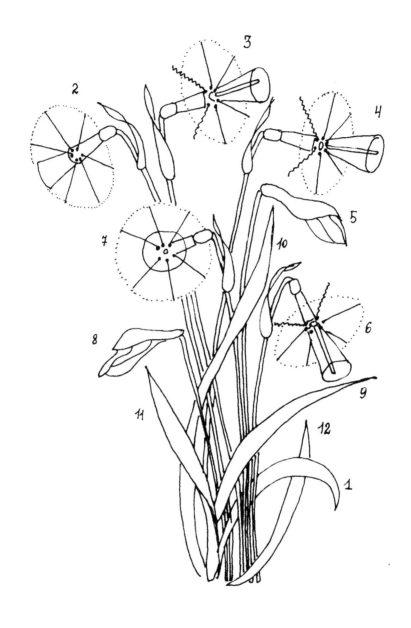

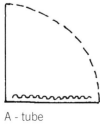

A - tube

B - perianth

You will need

Ribbon

Di van Niekerk's silk and organza ribbons

- 4 mm silk no. 36
- 4 mm silk no. 24
- 4 mm silk no. 137
- 7 mm silk no. 36
- 7 mm silk no. 54
- 32 mm silk no. 51

Needles

- Embroidery/crewel: size 9 and 10
- Quilting/betweens: size 9 and 10
- Chenille: size 18 and 20
- Tapestry: size 13

What else?

Background fabric

Pale cream Dupion silk fabric or silk-satin, large enough to fit in a 25 cm (10 inch) quilting hoop.

Backing fabric

Use another block of sheer organza, the same size as the background fabric.

Thread

Separate one strand from the six and work with one strand of thread unless suggested otherwise.

Rajmahal Art Silk

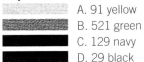

- A. 91 yellow
- B. 521 green
- C. 129 navy
- D. 29 black

DMC six-strand thread

- E. 840 brown

DMC Perlé 8

- F. 726 yellow

You will also need

- 25cm (10 inch) quilting hoop
- Pins and small, sharp embroidery scissors
- Black waterproof pigment ink pen with a fine tip
- Tracing paper; glue stick and clear liquid glue: see page 28
- Blue water-soluble pen
- 0.3 mm beading or fine stumpwork wire for little butterfly on page 45
- Optional: anti-fray agent – clear water-soluble liquid

Stitches used

Twisted ribbon stitch, twisted straight stitch, straight/stab stitch, French knot, ribbon stitch, padded ribbon stitch, padded straight stitch, double ribbon stitch

Prepare the design

For this design choose a soft cream Dupion silk, silk-stain or pure linen fabric. Trace the pattern on page 48 and see Getting started on pages 9 to 17. Place the fabric layers in your hoop as shown on page 11.

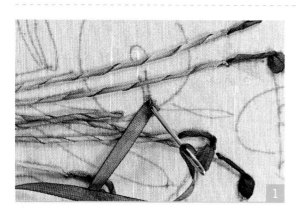

Make the stems

Narcissus stems consist of two parts: the lighter green stem made with 4 mm ribbon no. 36, and the upper, dark green neck and ovary made with 4 mm ribbon no. 24. Make the long stems first. Thread up with 4 mm ribbon no. 36 and, starting at the bottom, work upward following the pattern on page 48. Secure the tail at the back and then twist the ribbon to form a cylindrical stem. See Twisted straight stitch and Twisted ribbon stitch on pages 159 and 160. Insert needle to the back and cut the ribbon, leaving a short tail. With thread B, secure the ribbon at the back of your work. Use the same thread and make tiny stab stitches between the twirls of the ribbon to secure the stem onto your design.

Read page 25 for more about making long twisted stems. Start again at the bottom of the design and repeat until all the stems are made, working over the leaves which will be added a little later.

Hint: Hide the tails accurately just under the stem so that they is not visible through the light background fabric.

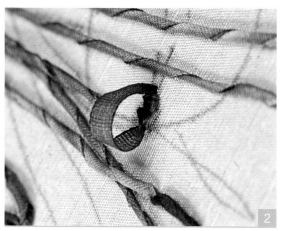

Form the dark ovary and neck with 4 mm ribbon no. 24. Make two or three folds in the ribbon as shown and, working from the right side, insert the needle through the folded ribbon and the fabric. Come up and make a small straight stitch.

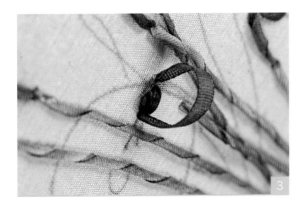

Gently pull the ribbon to the back. Make a second stitch on top – see Padded straight stitch in the stitch gallery on page 160. The second stitch is slightly longer to cover the first one.

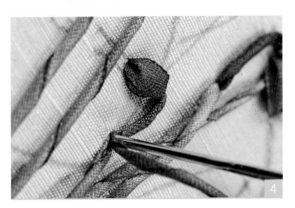

Come up to make a twisted ribbon stitch which will form the neck of the flower.

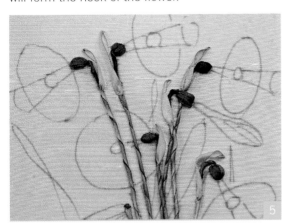

Form the pale cream spathes with 4 mm ribbon no. 137 and make ribbon stitch, twisting the needle once or twice before piercing the ribbon to take the needle to the back. To form a bend in the stitch use thread A or B and make tiny stab stitches to shape the stitch. See Shaping and securing stitches on page 21.

Make Narcissus leaves

Use 7 mm ribbon no. 36 and double ribbon stitch to make the leaves. Refer to the pattern as a guide and to Double ribbon stitch on page 23. Weave the needle under the stems where shown. Use a gentle tension; twist the needle to form twirled leaves.

Secure the tails on the reverse with thread B and use the same thread to secure the tips and the base of each leaf.

See Shaping and securing stitches on page 21. With the same thread B, make tiny stab stitches to secure the ribbon where it touches the fabric, placing stitches only where necessary.

Making the flowers

Use 7 mm ribbon no. 54 and make yellow perianths with several loose straight stitches to form a puffed dimensional bud. Use a gentle tension and work over a large needle or similar object to help raise the stitch off the surface.

Secure the stitch with tiny stab stitches and thread A. With 7 mm ribbon no. 36, make the green stitch that overlaps the yellow ones.

With 7 mm ribbon no. 54, use straight stitches to embroider four sepals/petals inside the oval as shown.

Work from the centre out and use thread A to secure the stitches so that they do not pull out of shape whilst you stitch.

With the same colour ribbon, make two free-standing sepals or petals. Come up from the back, and cut the ribbon to the desired length. With thread A, secure the tail at the back and use a glue stick or a tiny bit of transparent liquid glue along the upright edge on the right side. Allow time to dry and trim to form the rounded corners.

Flowers facing the other way are embroidered in ribbon or straight stitch, worked over a large needle or your fingertip so that the stitches are raised off the surface. See how the stitches have a convex shape? To achieve this, twist the ribbon on the wrong side to turn the stitch so that it has a convex shape on the right side of your design. Do this when you form each stitch.

Repeat these steps for all the Narcissus flowers, refer to the main picture on page 47 as a guide.

Make the orange perianth

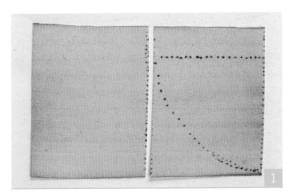

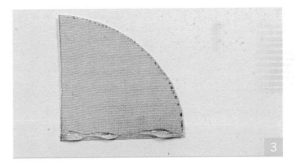

This is the most glamorous part of the flower and is made of 32 mm ribbon no. 51. Mark a section with a radius of 25 mm or 1 inch (A on page 48). Consider different options when cutting out the segment. I found the best was to match one side with the ribbon's edge.

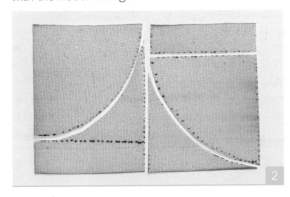

Add tiny glue dots along the edge of the segment and make a cone, using the glued edge to secure the shape as shown. Allow to dry.

Repeat for three more cones – there are four in this design. Trace the tiny perianth shape (B) on page 48 onto the same colour ribbon. Cut out and place it under the yellow sepals/petals of flower 2. Refer to the picture (top left) of this page as a guide. Use thread A to secure it onto your design with tiny stitches.

Secure each cone onto the yellow sepals/petals with tiny stab stitches and use thread A. With thread F, make a yellow pistil for each cone. Cut a length of thread, long enough to make the pistil and secure it.

Run the thread for the pistil through a glue stick. Allow to dry. Thread one glued pistil into the needle and from the right side, insert the needle to the back to form the pistil. Gently pull the needle back until you are happy with the position of the pistil. Secure at the back with tiny stab stitches and thread A. Repeat for all the cones.

Hint: If you like, make a paste of yellow fabric paint and thickener. Insert the point of the glued thread into the mixture to make a rounded end.

With thread E, form the ground at the base of the leaves using straight stitch.

You may wish to add a 3D butterfly. See the instructions for making butterflies on pages 45 – 46.

Poppies

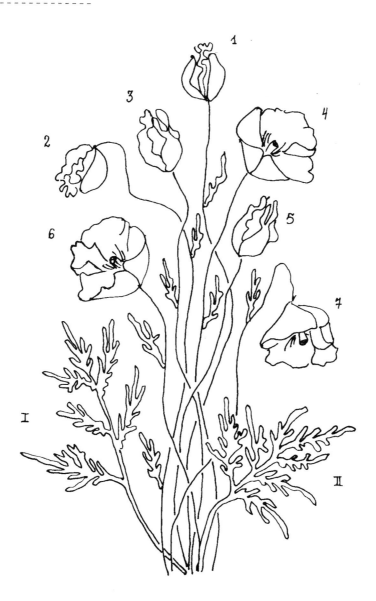

petal for open poppies

You will need

Ribbon

Di van Niekerk's silk organza ribbons

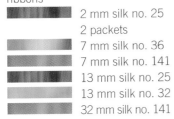 2 mm silk no. 25
2 packets
7 mm silk no. 36
7 mm silk no. 141
13 mm silk no. 25
13 mm silk no. 32
32 mm silk no. 141

Needles

- Embroidery/crewel: size 9 and 10
- Chenille: size 14 or 16
- Chenille: mixed pack sizes 18/22
- Chenille: size 28
- Tapestry: size 13

What else?
Background fabric

Pale cream Dupion silk fabric or silk-satin, large enough to fit in a 25 cm (10 inch) quilting hoop.

Backing fabric
Cream or white organza fabric, same size as above.

Thread

Separate one strand from the six and work with one strand of thread unless suggested otherwise.

Rajmahal Art Silk

A. 521 green
B. 29 black
C. 253 red
D. 311 brown
E. ecru
F. 44 yellow

DMC six-strand thread

G. 3364 green
H. 840 brown

Other
Wool fibre: green to fill the shapes, or use white toy filling.

You will also need

- 25 cm (10 inch) quilting hoop
- Pins and sharp embroidery scissors
- Old scissors or nail clippers to cut wire
- Black waterproof pigment ink pen with a fine tip
- Tracing paper
- Blue water-soluble pen
- Glue: glue stick and clear liquid glue, see page 16
- Q-tips or similar kind of cosmetic ear bud
- Copper wire or beading/stumpwork wire, 0.3 mm
- Bead, 10 mm (just over $\frac{3}{8}$ inch) for seed pod

Stitches used

Twisted straight stitch, twisted ribbon stitch, straight/stab stitch, ribbon stitch, running stitch, back stitch and looped back stitch

Prepare the design

For this design choose a soft cream Dupion silk, silk-satin or pure linen fabric. Trace the pattern on page 56 and see Getting started on pages 9 to 17. Place the fabric layers in your hoop as shown on page 11.

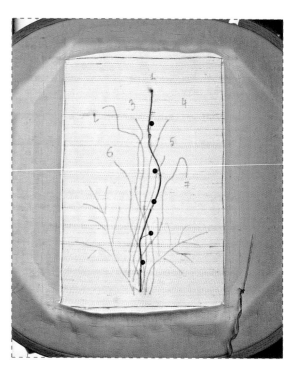

Make the stems

With 2 mm silk ribbon no. 25, make the stems in twisted straight stitch or use twisted ribbon stitch. For more details about twisted stems, refer to Making long twisted stems on page 25.

Work from the ground up. From the back of your work, come up and twirl the needle and ribbon to form a tightly coiled stem. Take the needle to the back again at the end of the stem, close to where the flower will be. Use a gentle tension and allow the ribbon to unwind at the back to prevent loops from forming. **Note:** Twist needle either clockwise or anti-clockwise depending on the direction you want the stem to bend.

secure it onto your design, only where necessary, working through all the layers. Leave parts of the twisted stem loose to imitate natural stems.

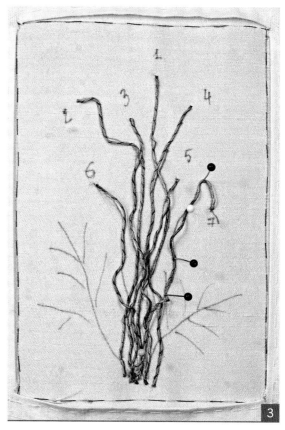

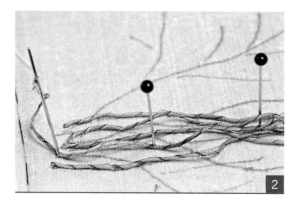

Use pins to hold the shape and twists of the stem and with thread A, make tiny stab stitches to

Make the leaves

Embroider the leaves with 2 mm ribbon no. 25 and use ribbon stitch. Work from the stem outwards and use a gentle tension so as not to flatten the leaves too much. Read About ribbon stitch on page 22.

You may want to dissolve some of the lines of the stem once embroidered. Use a Q-Tip, cotton ear bud or cosmetic stick: soak it in water and draw along the painted lines to wet the background fabric. If it is silk and the fabric dries, it stretches to form a beautiful flat surface. Read about Background fabric on page 10.

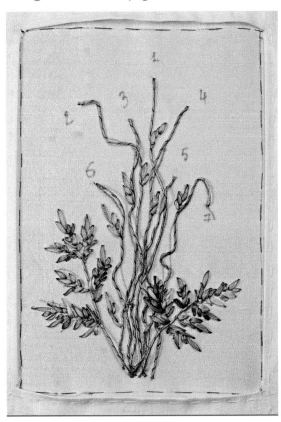

Make the ovaries

You will need three ovaries to complete the design. For each ovary, use 5 cm (2 inches) of 7 mm silk ribbon no. 36 and fold the ribbon in half lengthways. With thread A and tiny running stitches, close the sides of the shape. Use the large needle to turn the shape inside out and fill it with toy filling or green woolly fibre so that it is filled up to 1 cm (just over ⅜ inch) away from the opening.

With thread F, form the top of the ovary. Make stigmas with small straight and back stitches, working from inside the shape to get to the point. Spread stitches as rays. Make a row of back stitches below the rays.

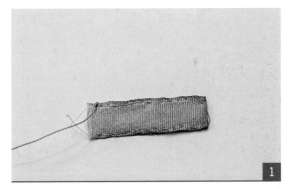

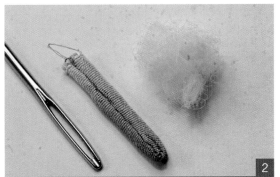

Make the stamens

Use two strands of thread B (40 cm or 16 inches) and make two rows of looped back stitches. Cut the loops. Wet the thread with a damp Q-Tip or cotton ear bud. Insert your scissors into each loop and pull it outwards as you cut. This will straighten the thread. Cut to desired length, being careful not to trim too short. Use the tips of your fingers to brush the stamens into shape. Place safely aside until later.

Make the buds

Take 7 mm ribbon no. 141 and refer to the pattern for the numbered shapes. Make bud 1 with two or three ribbon stitches. Work from the stem up and twist the ribbon once or twice to form loosely-made petals. Repeat for bud 2.

- -

Hint: To form the looped ends, don't pull the ribbon all the way through to the back and use a gentle tension whilst you stitch.

- -

Change to 7 mm ribbon no. 36 and, with the same stitch, make the green sepals around bud 1. Repeat for the sepals on bud 2. Make buds 3 and 5 in the same way: form loose and plump stitches and twirl the ribbon once before piercing it. Work with a gentle tension so as not to flatten the ribbon.

- -

Hint: If you find that your tension is too tight, work over a large needle or similar object when forming the stitches. Re-shape and secure the stitches with thread E or A.

- -

Make the open poppies

Make petals as described under Making the petals on page 33. Mark places on the fabric where petals will be embroidered. Take the tails through the fabric and secure on the reverse side with tiny stitches and thread C.

Hint: It is a good idea to spread the petals alternately: each opposite pair of petals occupies the same position. To insert a petal easily use a size 16 or 14 chenille needle which will make a large enough hole in the background fabric for the tails to be taken to the back. Secure on the reverse side with thread C or E and use tiny stitches.

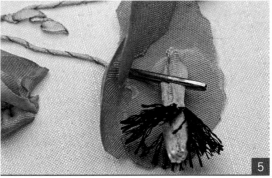

Insert an ovary, shape it and fix the tail with tiny stab stitches using thread A. The stitches are almost invisible. Secure the tail on the back of your work, ensuring that the tail lies under the poppy and is not visible through the background fabric.

Repeat for the other open poppies. Refer to the main picture on page 55.

Add grass at the base of the stems. Choose threads A and G for the green grass and use long straight stitches. Use thread D to add brown blades of grass between the green stitches. Mix green and brown threads for a natural effect.

With thread H, embroider several straight stitches to form the soil.

Note: To make this design more interesting and dimensional, make 3D poppies at different stages in their life cycle. These are made separately and then applied to the design. A 3D poppy can be added, or a seed pod, a spent flower or a blossoming bud. The step-by-step instructions are on page 33 to 42.

POPPIES

Chamomiles

Pattern size
12 CM X 15 CM
5" X 6"

bees   spider

You will need

Ribbon

Di van Niekerk's silk and organza ribbons

	4 mm silk no. 103 2 packets
	2 mm silk no. 103
	2 mm silk no. 132 2 packets
	2 mm silk no. 73
	2 mm silk no. 22
	2 mm silk no. 140
	2 mm silk no. 95 2 packets
	32 mm silk no. 32

Needles

- Embroidery/crewel: size 9 and 10
- Quilting/betweens: size 9 and 10
- Chenille: size 18, 20, 22 and 28 for metallic thread
- Tapestry: size 13

What else?

Background fabric and backing fabric

Pale cream or off-white Dupion silk fabric.
Organza backing fabric in white or cream – the same size as the Dupion silk above.

Thread and fibre

Separate one strand from the six and work with one strand of thread unless suggested otherwise.

DMC six-strand thread

	A. 208 medium lilac
	B. 209 lighter lilac
	C. 211 pale lilac
	D. 4045 variegated green
	E. 610 brown
	F. 520 green
	G. 3348 pale green

Rajmahal Art Silk

	H. 521 green
	I. 144 golden yellow
	J. 94 buttercup yellow
	K. 29 charcoal

Metallic thread

	L. Metallic silver thread

Fibre

Wool fibre: green, or use toy filling

You will also need

- 25 cm (10 inch) embroidery or quilting hoop
- 10 to 15 cm (4 to 6 inch) hoop for 3D flower
- Pins and tracing paper
- Black waterproof pigment ink pen with a fine tip
- Blue water-soluble pen
- Glue stick – see page 16
- Wire: see 3D Chamomiles on pages 30 to 32

Stitches used

Straight/stab stitch, fly stitch, split stitch, back stitch, split backstitch, running stitch, ribbon stitch, French knot, Turkey stitch, twisted/twirled straight stitch, twisted/twirled ribbon stitch and loop stitch

Prepare the design

For this design choose a soft cream Dupion silk, satin or pure linen fabric. Trace the pattern on page 66 and see Getting started on pages 9 to 17. Place the fabric layers in your hoop as shown on page 11.

Make the lavender in the background

Make the lavender flowers and stems. To create the feeling of space and depth, the six lavender flowers in the background are embroidered with thread. Make French knots, wrapping thread once around your needle for some petals and twice around your needle for others. Embroider the darkest colour first to form the depth of the flower. For this, use thread A and make several French knots along the stem, wrapping thread rather tightly to form small knots. Add the medium lilac knots on top with thread B, this time wrapping thread two or three times around your needle with a looser tension for a frilly knot. Finally, working over the previous layers, add the palest petals in thread C, wrapping thread two or three times around your needle.

Hint: For extra frilly knots, wrap thread very loosely around your needle.

To make the stems, use green thread F and, working from the ground up, make long straight stitches, referring to the pattern as a guide. Form the small green side stalks in straight or fly stitch. Make the large green leaves with the same thread; use fly stitches close together, making one stitch inside the other.

Hint: You could also use straight stitch, as shown, instead of fly stitch. Make them close together.

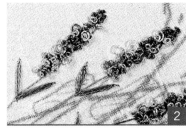

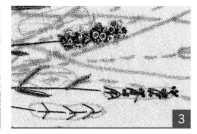

Make grass in the background

Add several straight stitches with thread D to form the grass in the background. Work from the ground upwards and note the bent blades of grass, which are made with two straight stitches.

Make the chamomile stems and leaves

Chamomiles form the midground of the composition. Use 2 mm ribbon no. 132 to make the stems and the leaves.

Stems are formed with long twisted straight stitches. Refer to Making long twisted stems on page 25 for information on how to make and fix the twisted stems onto your fabric.

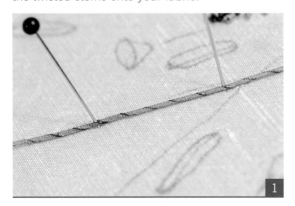

Leaves are made of loose, puffed ribbon stitch. Work from the stem outwards and use a pin or your fingertip to form curved leaves that are raised off the surface of the fabric. Read About ribbon stitch on page 22.

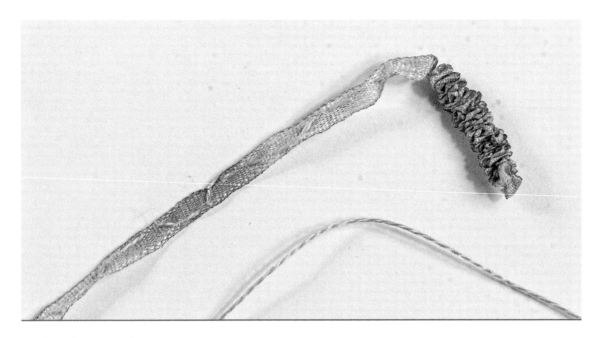

Make the meadow grass

For one flower head, you will need 30 cm (12 inches) of 2 mm ribbon no. 140. Fold the one end of the ribbon. Use one strand of thread G and make a knot at the long end. Insert needle into the fold on the ribbon; make small running stitches in a zigzag pattern along the length of the ribbon. Leave a tail on the ribbon and the thread. Gently shape the gathers to make a flower head of desired length. Make the stems with thread G and split stitch. Or you could use back stitch or split backstitch. Refer to the pattern as a guide for placement of stems.

Insert a chenille needle into the fabric and thread the tail of the flower head into it. Take the tail to the back with a gentle tension so as not to flatten the gathers. Use thread H to secure tail behind the flower head on the reverse side. On the right side, use a tiny stitch or two on the tip and the base of flower head to secure it. If necessary, make a stitch in the middle too.

Make five or six meadow grass flower heads, referring to the completed picture as a guide.

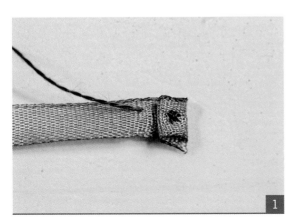

Make lavender in the foreground

Lavender in the foreground is made with ribbon and a thread as you did for the meadow grass. This way the flowers are loose and voluminous. Use 2 mm ribbon no. 73; you will need 20 cm or 8 inches of the ribbon for each flower head. Use a 55 cm (22 inch) length of thread B and make a knot at the long end.

Insert needle into the folded ribbon and gather the thread with small running stitches as you did for the meadow grass. Make a zigzag pattern with zigzags that are 2 cm (¾ inch) long.

Gather the ribbon to make a flower head of the desired length and attach it to the background as you did for the meadow grass.

Embroider very loose French knots with threads A, B and C, working over the ribbon flower head to add a frilly texture. Repeat for the other lavender flowers, referring to the completed picture on page 65 as a guide. There are four large flower heads in the foreground.

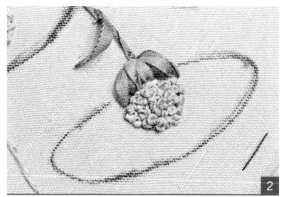

Make the green calyxes with 2 mm ribbon no. 132 and use ribbon stitch, working from the stem outwards. Form loose and puffed stitches that will add volume.

Use 2 mm green ribbon no. 22 to make lavender stems in twisted straight stitch as you did for the chamomile stems. Refer to the pattern as a guide. Lavender leaves are embroidered with the same ribbon and make loose, puffed leaves with ribbon stitch. If you like, use thread I and straight stitch to add fine grass between the leaves. Secure and re-shape leaves with the same thread (see page 21).

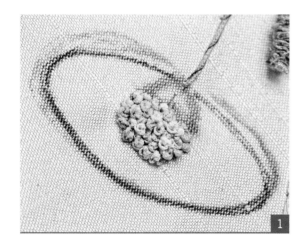

Make the white petals with 4 mm ribbon no. 103 and use straight stitch and loop stitch. Refer to the completed picture as a guide.

Make the chamomile flowers

Make the yellow stamens with 2 mm ribbon no. 95; use French knots wrapped tightly once around the needle. Fill the shape with knots. This is the first layer. To add volume, make a second layer of extra tight French knots, working on top of the first layer (come up between the knots), wrapping ribbon around needle as you did before. Insert needle back between the knots.

Hint: When making loop stitches use two needles to make sure the final petals are of similar size. Embroider all the looped petals, adding straight stitches randomly for a more natural appearance.

These chamomile flowers will look almost lifelike if the loops are pasted together. Spread a small amount of glue evenly over the inside of the loop using the tip of the needle. Press lightly with your fingertips and try to align the edges.

With 2 mm ribbon no. 103, embroider the little white buds in ribbon stitch. Refer to the picture of the completed piece as a guide.

Make the brown soil

Use thread E and make the soil at the base of the flowers in straight stitch. Refer to picture of the completed piece as a guide.

Make the little bees and a spider

Little insects always add charm and they are easy to make. Refer to page 44 for how to make the bees and to page 43 for a spider.

Add a 3D flower

You may wish to create even more volume by adding a 3D chamomile to your design – such fun to make, and so realistic! See pages 30 to 33 for the instructions. To inspire you, here are more close-up pictures of this charming design.

Rose wreath

Pattern size

15 CM X 15 CM
6" X 6"

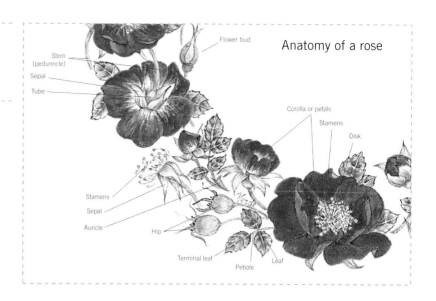

Anatomy of a rose

Flower bud

Stem (pedunncle)

Sepal

Tube

Corolla or petals

Stamens

Disk

Stamens

Sepal

Auricle

Hip

Terminal leaf

Petiole

Leaf

ROSE WREATH

You will need

Ribbon

Di van Niekerk's silk and organza ribbons

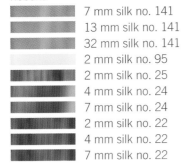

7 mm silk no. 141
13 mm silk no. 141
32 mm silk no. 141
2 mm silk no. 95
2 mm silk no. 25
4 mm silk no. 24
7 mm silk no. 24
2 mm silk no. 22
4 mm silk no. 22
7 mm silk no. 22

Needles

- Embroidery/crewel: size 9 and 10
- Quilting/betweens: size 9 and 10
- Chenille: size 18, 20, 22, 24 and 28
- Tapestry: size 13

What else?
Background fabric

Cream to off-white Dupion silk fabric.

Organza backing fabric

White or cream – the same size as the background above.
A block of white fabric for a dust cover – similar size as background fabric above.

Thread

Separate one strand from the six and work with one strand of thread unless suggested otherwise.

DMC six-strand thread

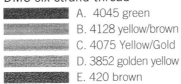

A. 4045 green
B. 4128 yellow/brown
C. 4075 Yellow/Gold
D. 3852 golden yellow
E. 420 brown

Rajmahal Art Silk

F. 521 green
G. 91 light yellow
H. 255 red

Beads
Any colour:

- 4 mm x 25 pieces
- 6 mm x 2 pieces
- 8 mm x 2 pieces

You will also need

- 25 cm (10 inch) embroidery or quilting hoop
- Pins, tracing paper and a blue water-soluble pen
- Black waterproof pigment ink pen with a fine tip
- Very sharp light green pencil
- Glue stick and transparent glue – see What else do I need? on page 16

Stitches used

Straight/stab stitch, running stitch, stem stitch, ribbon stitch, French knot, looped back stitch, twisted/twirled straight stitch, pistil stitch and twisted/twirled ribbon stitch

Prepare the design

For this design choose a soft cream Dupioni silk, satin or pure linen fabric. See the Getting started on pages 9 to 17. Collect all items needed for the project, following the list on the previous page.

Note: This design is rather intricate, with numerous little details which should be carefully transferred onto the fabric.

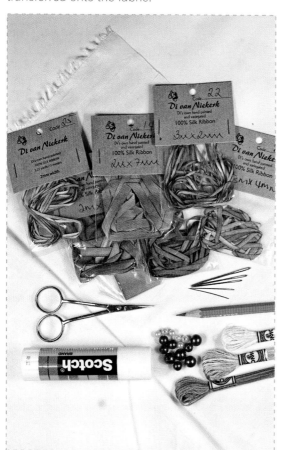

Prepare the dust cover

The design has a diameter of 15 cm (6 inches). As mentioned on the list, use a white block of fabric for the dust cover.

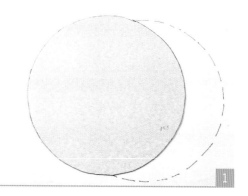

With a piece of cardboard make a stencil as follows: draw a circle with a 17.5 cm (7 inch) diameter and cut the cardboard circle out. Place it in the centre of the cover fabric and use a water-soluble pen to draw the shape onto the dust cover.

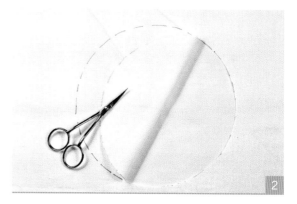

Cut out the "window" in the dust cover fabric.

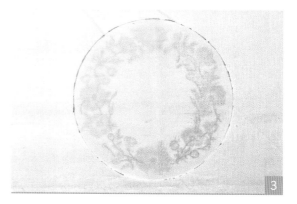

Match the background fabric and cover fabric, then secure with pins.

Place the paper pattern under the background to ensure that the window is large enough and that the design elements are not hidden under the cover fabric.

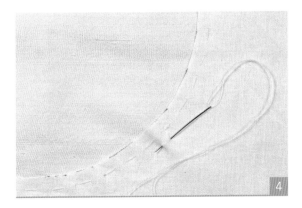

Fix background and cover fabrics with straight or running stitch, leaving a 5 to 7 mm (¼ inch) seam.

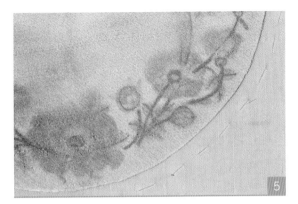

Place the pattern under the background fabric and accurately transfer the main lines (stems, petioles, middle of the roses) with a very sharp light green pencil. The green colour is friendly to designs with numerous leaves and will hardly be visible when your embroidery is completed.

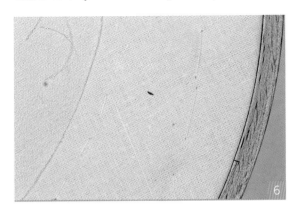

Place the layers into the hoop (including an organza backing fabric if using one) and stretch firmly to remove all the creases. Fold the edges

and tack them out of the way (with running or straight stitch) for a convenient embroidery process.

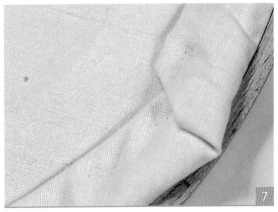

Reverse side.

Embroidery process

This charming design can conveniently be divided into four main segments which are connected by the large roses. I suggest that you start on any quarter-circle to try out the stitches and techniques and to familiarise yourself with the sequence of the embroidery process, which repeats in the other quarter-circles. Photos will show how the main elements are embroidered, and you decide whether you will embroider segments from the beginning to the end, or whether you will embroider similar elements in each segment. Any option will lead to the same result – your magnificent piece of art!

Stems and petioles

I usually start with those elements that form the background of the design – stems and petioles.

Alternate between the 4 mm green ribbons as follows:

- **For the rose stems:** choose 4 mm ribbon no. 22 or no. 24.
- **For the bud stems:** use 4 mm ribbon no. 22.
- **For the stems of the open roses:** use 4 mm ribbon no. 24.

The design will have the same colour combination for all the quarter-circles.

Use long twisted straight or ribbon stitches to make perfectly formed stems. Read more about making long twisted stems on page 25. Use thread A for the petioles; make short stem stitches according to the design.

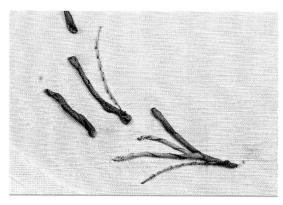

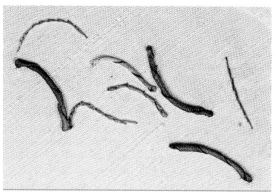

Tubes

At every stage of life each rose flower has a tube. Use 4 mm beads to make all the tubes.

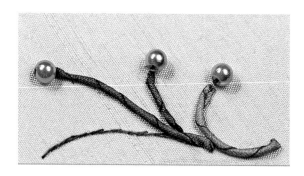

Attach them with several stitches using the green thread F.

Make two straight stitches with 7 mm ribbon no. 22 and firmly wrap the beads. All the tubes are made in the same way.

Hint: Make sure each side of the bead is covered and the bead is not visible.

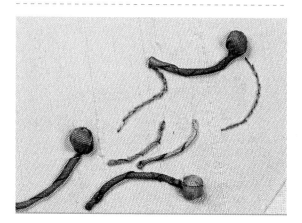

Rose buds with closed sepals

Rose buds with closed sepals are made in the same way as follows: Attach a 4 mm bead. With 7 mm ribbon no. 141

Make two straight stitches, working with a gentle tension. These stitches are not as tight as the green ones.

Form a bud by making two stitches alongside and overlapping one another. The bead underneath helps to create volume.

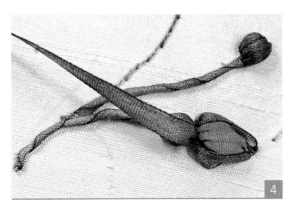

Take a 4 mm ribbon no. 22. Refer to About ribbon stitch on page 22. Right ribbon stitch on the left side of the bud and left ribbon stitch on the right side of the bud will gently cover the sides of the bud.

Embroider another ribbon stitch (with needle in the centre of the stitch) to "close" the bud. Make the sharp end of the sepals with thread A and make three straight stitches for lifelike results.

Using beads gives a better result when compared with using only ribbon stitches. It will retain the form of the elements and add volume to your work.

This photograph demonstrates the difference: the upper bud was made with only three ribbon stitches using 4 mm ribbon no. 22. The one below has a bead inside.

A bead inside the buds can be substituted with a green French knot. Wrap ribbon once or twice around your needle. You decide which method suits you best.

Rose bud with open sepals

Use 7 mm ribbon no. 141 and embroider very loose left, right and central ribbon stitches. Twist the needle once before piercing the ribbon with your needle. Form a bud with three stitches.

With 4 mm ribbon no. 22 embroider sepals on the background, making sharp ends with thread A, as you did before. Make the loose, free-standing ribbon tails for green sepals as shown under Making free-standing ribbon tails on page 27. Make a knot on the back and pull the ribbon through to the right side. Cut a tail 8 to 10 mm (³⁄₈ inch) and make sharp ends by cutting the ribbon. Add a bit of transparent glue to prevent the silk ribbon from fraying.

Leaves

- Petioles are thinner than the stems, so they are embroidered with thread A.
- When embroidering leaves please remember that the terminal leaf is the largest one; all other leaf pairs are smaller the closer they are to the auricle.
- Use 7 mm ribbon no. 24 for a terminal leaf: make a loose ribbon stitch about 10 mm (just over ³⁄₈ inch) long. The next pair of leaves is embroidered with the same 7 mm ribbon no. 24, but the leaves are shorter: 7 to 8 mm (a bit over ¼ inch) in length.
- For smaller leaf pairs use 4 mm ribbon no. 24. The stitches are 5 to 6 mm (just over ³⁄₁₆ inch) long. Embroider them according to the pattern with loose, puffed ribbon stitches. Use a gentle tension so as not to flatten the stitch. Auricles are made with 2 mm ribbon no. 22 and using straight or twisted ribbon stitch.

Roses with open petals

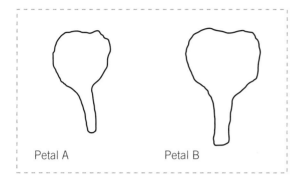

Petal A   Petal B

According to the design, cut out one or two petals A from 13 mm ribbon no. 141. Trace the template on the ribbon and when placing, note colour variations on the ribbon for lifelike effects. Set aside.

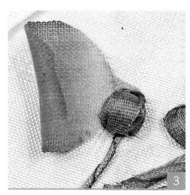

Make stems with 4 mm ribbon no. 22 and use twisted straight stitch. Attach a 4 mm bead for the tube and cover the bead with 7 mm ribbon no. 22 (two stitches). Refer to page 80 for instructions on covering the bead. Insert the tail of the petal in a large needle as shown and take it to the reverse side. Fix the tail on the reverse with thread G and tiny stitches. Be sure to hide the tails so that they will lie under the rose and not be visible through the light background fabric. Repeat and make more petals depending on the design. Add some glue and slightly curl the edges by rolling the ribbon gently around a large needle.

Embroider stamens with thread B: make loose French knots and pistil stitches, wrapping thread once or twice around your needle.

Roses with dropped-off petals (spent roses)

Embroider open-standing sepals with 4 mm ribbon no. 22, making sharp ends with thread A, as you did before. Make the loose, free-standing ribbon tails for green sepals as shown under Making free-standing ribbon tails on page 27. Make a knot on the back and pull the ribbon through to the right side. Cut a tail 8 to 10 mm and make sharp ends by cutting the ribbon. Add a bit of transparent glue to prevent the silk ribbon from fraying.

Make stems with 4 mm ribbon no. 22 and twisted straight stitch, as you did before. Attach a 4 mm bead and make a tube; cover the bead with 7 mm ribbon no. 22 (two straight stitches).

Embroider stamens with thread C. Make loosely wrapped French knots with one to two wraps around your needle. For longer stamens, use pistil stitch, wrapping thread once or twice around your needle.

Make sepals with 4 mm ribbon no. 22; form sharp ends with thread A and straight stitch.

Form free-standing sepals with 4 mm ribbon no. 22 as you did for the rose buds on page 82, steps 4 and 5. Trim the ends to make sharp points and apply glue to the ribbon ends to prevent fraying.

Embroider leaves with 7 mm and 4 mm ribbon no. 24 and use loose, puffed ribbon stitch as you did for the other leaves.

Embroider auricle with 2 mm ribbon no. 22. Refer to page 82 under Leaves.

Rose hips

Depending on the design, we'll make hips of two sizes with 8 mm or 6 mm beads.

For 8 mm beads: Use the 32 mm ribbon no. 141 and mark a circle with a diameter of 24 mm (almost an inch), leaving a 3 mm (almost 1/8 inch) seam. Cut out the circle.

For 6 mm beads: Use the 32 mm ribbon no. 141 and mark a circle with a diameter of 20 mm ($^{25}/_{32}$ inch), leaving a 3 mm (almost 1/8 inch) seam. Cut out the circle.

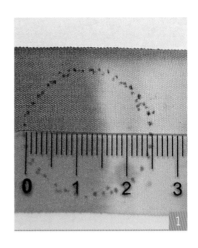

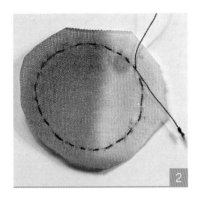

Use thread H with a knot at the long end and make small running stitches on the marked line.

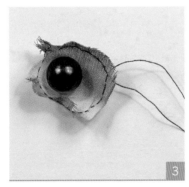

Pull the threads to gather slightly. Place the bead inside.

Fold seams and secure them with thread H, evenly spreading the folds.

The covered rose hip.

Embroider French knots over the top of the hip with thread B and thread E. Make small knots, wrapping thread once or twice around your needle.

Pull 2 mm ribbon no. 25 through the ribbon as shown and secure the tail with thread B or E. Leave tails 10 mm (just over 3/8 inch) long.

Trim to form sharp ends and apply transparent glue on the edges to prevent them from fraying.

Add some glue to the inside part of the sepals and slightly press them together as shown. Allow to dry. Secure the rose hips to your design with thread H or G, or use thread F.

The roses

There are two kinds of fully open roses in this design. The smaller rose has five petals and the large rose has eight.

Rose with five petals

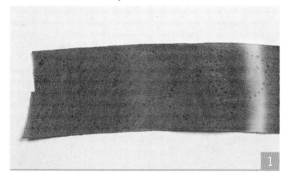

Five-petal roses are comparatively small, so use 13 mm ribbon no. 141. Trace petal A on page 83 with dotted lines with water-soluble pen and cut it out. Use the ribbon colour variation to its best advantage as shown above.

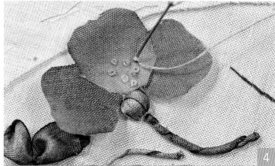

Cut out the petals and apply transparent glue to the edges to prevent fraying. Allow to dry. Secure the tails of three petals, as you did for roses with open petals on page 83.

Use thread B to embroider stamens with loose French knots, as you did before.

Embroider sepals; add sharp points with straight stitches and thread A or F.

Add free-standing sepals where necessary for the design. Form them with 4 mm ribbon no. 22 and refer to the rose buds on page 82.

Trim the ends to make sharp points and apply glue to the ribbon ends to prevent fraying.

Gently touch the edge of each petal with the glue stick; curl the edge with a needle. Allow to dry.

Rose with eight petals

Eight-petal roses have large and small petals, so we'll use both 32 mm and 13 mm ribbon no. 141 for different petals.

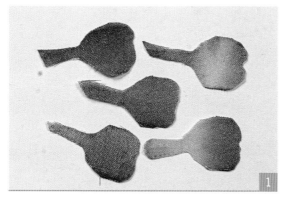

Trace the petal templates on page 83 for small (A) and large (B) petals and cut them out. Use ribbon colour variations to their best advantage to form interesting, lifelike petals.

Touch the two edges with glue stick and gently curl the edge of each petal with the needle as shown below.

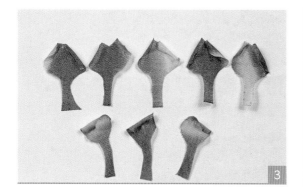

Now you have all the petals ready to embroider a large rose.
Note: Small petals are rolled up on one side. Do not worry about dots – they will disappear in 1 to 2 hours.

Mark dots on the fabric with the water-soluble pen to indicate placement and add the large petals first. Insert the large needle into the background and take the tail to the back, securing it as you did for the other roses. Add three small petals inside.

Embroider stamens with thread B and thread D, like you did before, using French knots with one to three wraps.

Make a large yellow disk with 2 mm ribbon no. 95; make a French knot, wrapping ribbon two or three times around your needle.

To make petals look more lifelike, use thread H and re-shape the form of the petals with tiny stab stitches. Petals will lift up differently and give the illusion of a real rose. Refer to Securing and shaping stitches on page 21 for more information.

Rose reverse side

Mark dots on the fabric with the water-soluble pen to indicate the position of the sepals in the next step. Add the large petals first.

Attach a 4 mm bead with thread F to make a tube.

Wrap it with two straight stitches using 7 mm ribbon no. 22.

Make a stem with 4 mm ribbon no. 22; add free-standing tails to make sepals.

Trim edges of the sepals so that they are sharp and apply transparent glue to fix them.

The completed reverse side.

Stamens

To make stamens you will need 50 cm (20 inches) of thread C. Process each thread with glue stick (just pull threads through the glue one by one) and allow to dry.

With this thread, embroider several looped back stitches, making loops 7 to 8 mm ($^5/_{16}$ inch) high. Cut the loops.

Embroider a disk with 2 mm ribbon no. 95 and make several stitches if necessary.

Cut thread where necessary to make stamens of desired height.

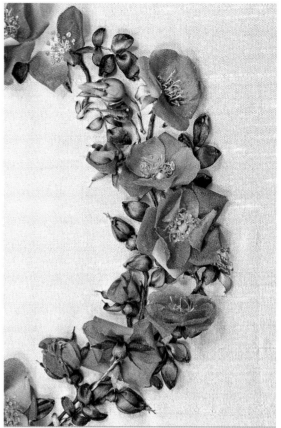

Strawberry blossoms

You will need

Ribbon

Di van Niekerk's silk and organza ribbons

	32 mm silk no. 147
	38 mm organza no. 147
	25 mm organza no. 139
	32 mm silk no. 146
	4 mm silk no. 19
	4 mm silk no. 24
	7 mm silk no. 104
	7 mm silk no. 33
	32 mm silk no. 33

Needles

- Embroidery/crewel: size 9 or 10
- Chenille: size 18, 20 and 22

Thread and fibre

Separate one strand from the six and work with one strand of thread unless suggested otherwise.

DMC six-strand thread

	A. 3364 green
	B. 451 brown
	C. 372 golden green
	D. 676 yellow

Rajmahal Art Silk

	E. 256 antique red

Kreinik Blending Filament

	F. 032 pearl

Fibres

- Wool fibre: medium green and dark green; watermelon pink; medium brown and pale yellow
- Silk fibre: pale green and pale blue

What else?

Background fabric

Off-white to pale cream silk-satin or Dupion silk fabric large enough to fit in a 25 cm (10 inch) quilting hoop.

Backing fabric

Cream or white organza, as large as background fabric above.

You will also need

- Anti-fray agent – clear water-soluble liquid
- Black waterproof pigment ink pen with a fine tip
- 25 cm (10 inch) quilting hoop
- Pins, tracing paper and sharp 2B pencil
- Blue water-soluble pen
- Q-tips or similar type of ear bud

Stitches used

Couching, fly stitch; straight/stab stitch, French knot, running stitch, ribbon stitch and twisted/twirled straight stitch

Prepare the design

For this design I chose a soft cream silk-organza fabric and placed a similar shade of silk-satin behind the organza to support it. Dupion silk, satin or pure linen fabric is also a good choice. Trace pattern onto the background fabric with a blue water-soluble pen.

- -

Hint: To prevent marks in your book, trace the pattern onto tracing paper first. Place the fabric in your hoop as shown on page 11.

Diagram A

Make stems and branches

Refer to diagram B below and make the stems and branches. Use all six strands of thread A. Place strands on fabric and couch in place with one strand of matching thread. Space couching stitches about 5 mm (³⁄₁₆ inch) apart. Use three strands of thread A and three strands of thread B on the same size 22 chenille needle and make V-shaped stems in fly stitch. Use straight stitch for the straight stems.

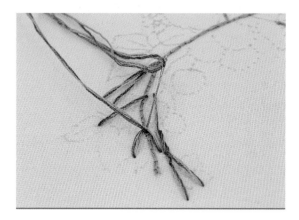

Hint: The formation of the stems and branches is essential – this is the framework on which you will be building your design. However, most of these stems will be covered by strawberries and leaves, so do not stress too much about neatness or exact placement thereof.

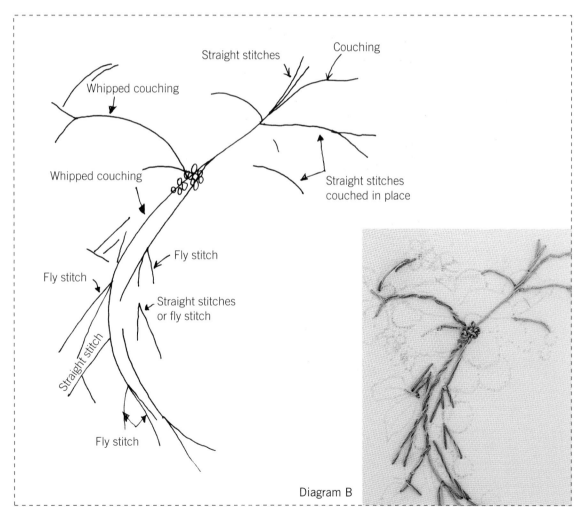

Straight stitches

Couching

Whipped couching

Whipped couching

Straight stitches couched in place

Fly stitch

Fly stitch

Straight stitches or fly stitch

Straight stitch

Fly stitch

Diagram B

Add a few French knots: wrap thread twice around the needle. Insert needle under and over the couched stem for an interesting effect – see Whipped couching on page 157.

Make strawberries

Strawberries are made with circular shapes of ribbon that are filled with woolly fibre to create the rounded shapes. Use a sharp pencil and trace six of the B (pink) circles onto silk ribbon no. 147 and six of the A (green) circles onto organza ribbon no. 147. **Note:** Draw some circles onto yellow/green part of the ribbon, others onto the red part (which will be used for the ripe strawberries).

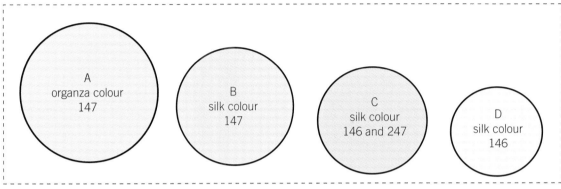

A
organza colour
147

B
silk colour
147

C
silk colour
146 and 247

D
silk colour
146

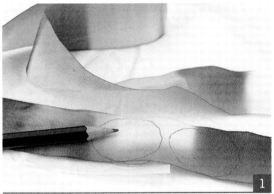

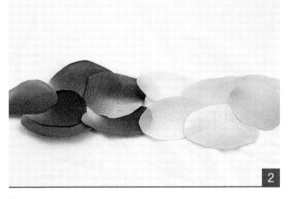

Draw four or five of the C (orange) circles onto silk no. 146 or 147. **Note:** These circles should have bits of pink showing alongside the yellow. Draw two D (yellow) circles onto silk ribbon no. 146.

Cut out the shapes as shown.

Hint: If folds on the ribbon are bothering you, press with a steam iron on a silk setting.

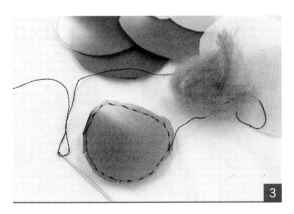

Take a reddish silk (no. 147) B circle made and thread up with the E thread. Make a knot at the long end. Form a circle of running stitches about 2 mm ($\frac{1}{16}$ inch) as shown.

Place a ball of the pink fibre into the centre and gather the thread to form a ball.

Work stitches across the opening to hold the fibre and end off. Take an organza circle A and repeat running stitch along the edge, as before.

Gather slightly and place the silk ball inside the organza shape as shown.

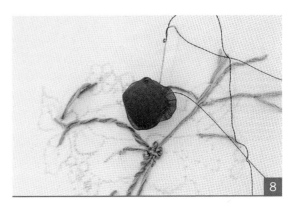

Gather thread and work thread across the opening to close it. With tiny stitches secure the strawberry onto the fabric, working along the edge of the shape through all the layers.

Hint: Use the blunt end of a chenille needle to push the loose bits of organza under the shape to neaten the edge. Use tiny stitches along the edge to shape and to neaten.

Make the tiny specks (achenes)

Use small straight stitches, working with a loose tension so as not to flatten the strawberry.

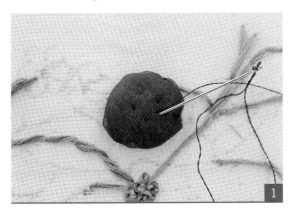

Hint: If you angle the needle through the woolly fibre as shown, the shape will flatten even less. Once completed, take the needle to the back and end off.

Make the silk leaves

Small strawberry leaves – draw two or three of each onto silk colour 33.

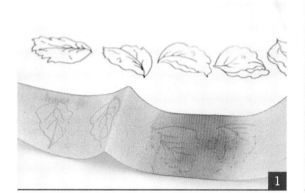

Take the 32 mm ribbon no. 33 and, with a blue water-soluble pen, trace two or three shapes from the template above. Cut out the shapes and use the black pigment ink pen to draw the veins onto the leaf. Apply water-soluble anti-fray agent onto the entire shape and allow time to dry.

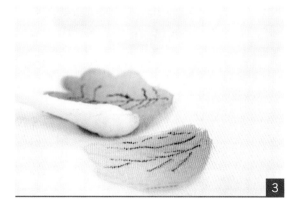

Dip an ear bud into water and dampen the edge of the leaf to remove the blue marks. Allow time to dry.

Use thread A and tiny straight stitches to secure a silk leaf onto the fabric as shown. Allow the edges of the shape to stand free.

Add five other leaves as shown. Working from the stem outwards and using tiny straight/stab stitches through all the layers, make two or three stitches one top of another to secure each shape. **Note:** The edges and tip of the leaves are lifted off the surface.

See how one of the leaves was secured along the central vein with small straight stitches? I did this to flatten this leaf onto the fabric.

Add shadows

Use a small piece of dark green fibre (about the size of a pea), teasing it out to form a flatter surface. Use the blunt end of a large needle to insert fibre between the leaves and under the strawberry. Add a piece of medium green to create more shadow and to help lift leaves up and off your design.

Use green thread A to secure the fibre with small straight stitches placed here and there – the fibre should not be flattened too much and the stitches are only necessary to hold fibre in place. Add a small piece of brown fibre too.

Make the green calyx and stem

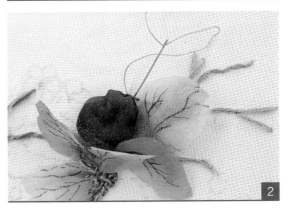

Thread up with 7 mm ribbon no. 33 and make the calyx of the strawberry with ribbon stitch. Use a gentle tension so as not to flatten the stitch. Make three or four stitches close together. More stitches will be added later.

Make the stem with the same ribbon and twisted straight stitch, twisting the ribbon before inserting needle under the leaf and taking it to the back of your work. Hold the stem as you take the ribbon to the back to form a softly curved shape. Use thread A and tiny stab stitches to secure the stem – place stitches only where necessary; work with a gentle tension so as not to flatten the stem.

Use the shiny thread F and add some more specks (achenes) on the strawberry with tiny straight stitches.

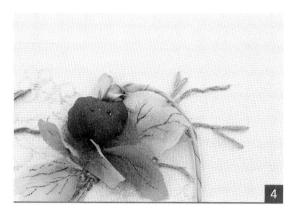

Make more strawberries

Make a second strawberry as you did the first with silk and organza shapes. Secure with tiny stitches, shaping and neatening the edge as you stitch.

Make a third strawberry in the same way, and a fourth and a fifth. See how the ripest strawberries are made with the reddest circles?

Use the pale green fibre, placing it between the strawberries to build texture.

Secure with thread A or C and tiny stab stitches. Place stitches only where necessary – the woolly texture shouldn't be too flat. Pull the fibre gently to add colour along the edge of the design. Use one or two stitches to secure as you did before.

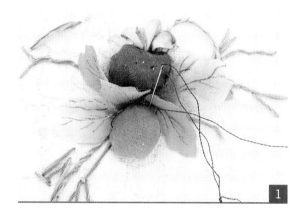

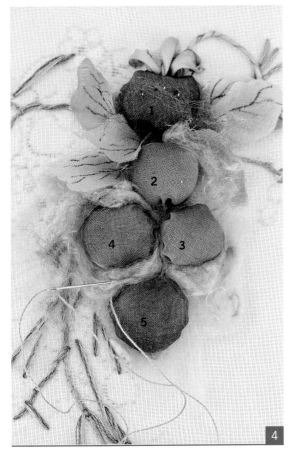

Add a sixth strawberry on the top left-hand side as shown in the photograph.

Hint: Use circles with a lot of red for this ripe strawberry. With thread A, make green specks (achenes) on the strawberries as you did before. Add the darker specks with thread E and shiny highlights with thread F.

Use 7 mm ribbon no. 33 and make the green calyxes in ribbon stitch, as you did before. Form the stem in twisted straight stitch. Secure with thread A and tiny straight/stab stitches. Add more stems, working from the strawberries downward.

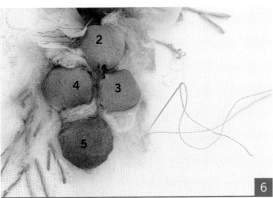

Make organza and silk leaves

Trace the leaf shapes onto the 25 mm organza ribbon no. 139. Cut out and secure onto design with thread C and little stab stitches.

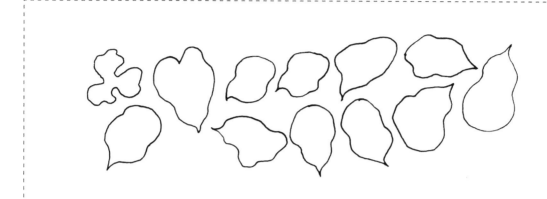

Hint: It is not necessary to use an anti-fray agent for the organza leaves. Make the veins with the same thread and use straight stitch. Add more organza leaves along the outer edge of the design – these leaves create interesting shadows. Insert a bit of brown fibre between the strawberries for dark shadows.

1

Add a few green silk leaves as you did before and secure with straight stitch, allowing the tips and edges to be lifted up off the surface.

Make the yellow strawberries

Use the yellow/pink silk circles C and make four or five half-ripe strawberries.
Note: These strawberries do not need organza circles to cover them. Make running stitch along the edge with thread D and use the pale yellow fibre to fill the shape. Secure three strawberries onto the lower section of your design. Add a fourth on the top left-hand side. If you like, you can add a fifth strawberry alongside, but wait until your design is completed, and then you decide whether to add it or not.

Optional: Only once your embroidery is completed, after the last step, you can use the pale blue silk fibre: gently tear a piece and tease it out to form a thin sheet. Place along the edge of the design to add soft background shadows. Secure onto your design with thread F, placing the stitches only where necessary.

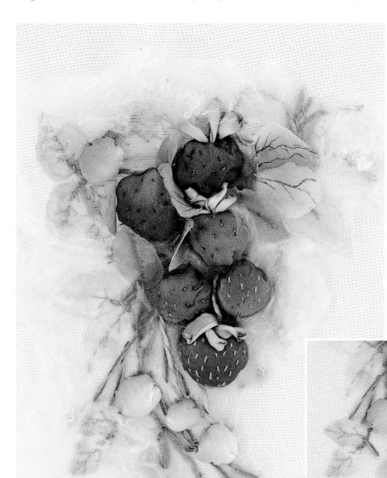

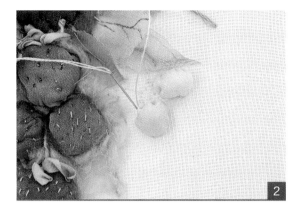

With the two smallest yellow silk circles D and thread D, make two unripe strawberries. Use the pale yellow fibre for the filling. Secure onto the right-hand side of the design.

The final detail

Use 7 mm silk ribbon no. 104 and make the strawberry blossoms in ribbon stitch, working from the centre outwards. With thread D make small French knots in the centre, wrapping thread three times around your needle. There are three blossoms at the top and two on the left. See the main picture on page 93.

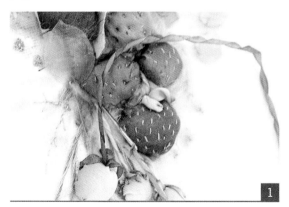

Use 4 mm ribbon no. 24 and make dark green stems in twisted straight stitch and calyxes in ribbon stitch, as you did before.

Use a gentle tension as you make the green sepals and leaves – if necessary, place a large tapestry needle under the stitch as you form it. This will help hold the shape when you take the ribbon to the back of your work.

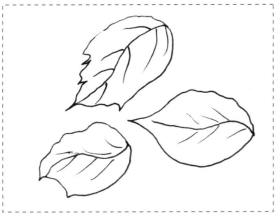

Trace the three leaf shapes onto 32 mm green silk no. 33. Trace three more onto 25 mm organza no. 139. Draw veins onto the silk shapes with black pen and apply anti-fray agent as you did before. Place an organza leaf on top of a silk one; insert between the strawberries as shown. With thread C, make stab stitches to secure. Repeat for the second leaf and the third, using both the silk and organza leaves – the organza leaf is placed on top of the silk one before you secure them between the strawberries.

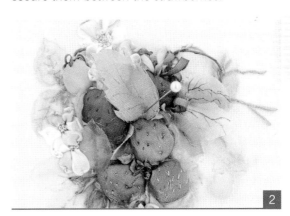

Add a bit of dark green fibre between the leaves to create dark shadows. Add some more pale green silk fibre (and some pale blue, if you like) on the outer edge of your design. Secure with thread C or F. Use a cotton ear bud: dip it into water and wet any areas with blue marks to dissolve them.

Ring of daisies

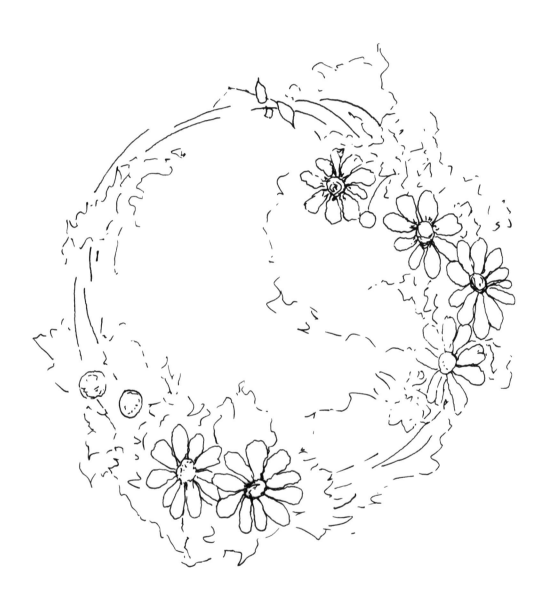

You will need

Ribbon

Di van Niekerk's silk and organza ribbons

7 mm silk no. 115
13 mm silk no. 99
32 mm silk no. 140
7 mm silk no. 123
7 mm silk no. 114

Findings: A small green or pale pink shell or a piece of precious stone, a special bead or a pearl (whatever you fancy)

Needles

- Embroidery/crewel: size 9 or 10
- Quilting/betweens: size 9 or 10
- Chenille: size 16 and 18
- Tapestry: size 13

Thread and fibre

Separate one strand from the six and work with one strand of thread unless suggested otherwise.

Rajmahal Art Silk

A. 45 golden yellow
B. 200 baby pink
C. 201 baby blue
D. 171 light brown

DMC six-strand thread

E. 3013 light green

Fibres

- Wool fibre: blue-green; dark green; powder blue; grey-green
- Silk fibre: pale green
- Silk paper: medium green – 5 cm (2 inch) block

What else?
Background fabric
Pale cream silk-satin or Dupion silk, large enough to fit in a 25 cm (10 inch) quilting hoop.
Optional: Place a layer of sheer organza (similar shade and size) on top for an interesting effect.

Backing fabric
Use another block of sheer organza, the same size as the background fabric.

You will also need

- 25 cm (10 inch) quilting hoop
- Pins and small, sharp embroidery scissors
- Black waterproof pigment ink pen with a fine tip
- Tracing paper, Pritt (or similar) glue stick: see page 16
- Blue water-soluble pen, small glass of water
- Sharp 2B pencil
- Optional: anti-fray agent – clear water-soluble liquid

Stitches used

Split stitch, stem stitch, split back stitch, loop stitch, running stitch, straight/stab stitch, French knot, ribbon stitch and padded ribbon stitch

Prepare the design

For this project I used a silk-satin background – the softest cream with a tinge of grey – and placed a similar shade of sheer organza fabric on top. For the backing fabric I used an additional block of organza. All three blocks of fabric are the same size: large enough to fit into a 25 cm or 10 inch hoop.

Hint: For round patterns it is often easier to place all the layers in the hoop first, pull the fabric taut as a drum and pin the corners out of the way. Trace the pattern onto a sheet of tracing paper and tape the tracing against the backing fabric, right side facing the fabric. Use a round box and cover the lid with white fabric or paper. Place the hoop on top of the box so that the tracing fits snugly against the fabric. Use a sharp pencil to trace the pattern. Remove the tracing.

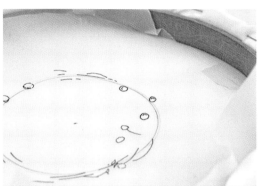

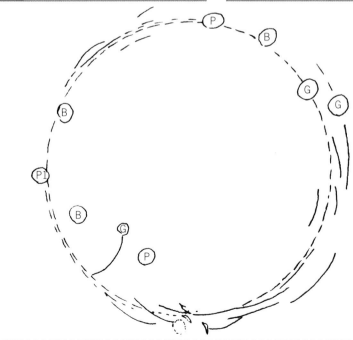

P – Pink
P1 – Start here
B – Blue
G – Green

Embroider the circle

Use two strands of thread A and, by stitching through all the layers, make the circular pattern in split stitch. You could also choose stem or split back stitch. On sections of the circle which will lie under the daisies, you could use running stitch to save time.

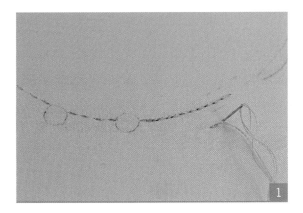

Make the daisies

Make the first pink daisy (P1 on pattern). Use an awl or large chenille needle to make eight to ten holes in your fabric, working around the pencilled circles. Thread up with 7 mm ribbon no. 115. Use a short length of ribbon to prevent fraying – 15 cm (6 inches) is a good length for this ribbon. Come up in the centre, leave a tail and pin it out of the way. You will secure the tails a little later.

Make four loops, working over a spare tapestry needle. Form neat petals about 1 cm (just over $\frac{3}{8}$ inch) long. Take the needle to the back, cut off excess ribbon, leaving a short tail. Use the B thread to secure the tails and the loops: stitch along the base of each loop with a few tiny stab stitches. Repeat and make an additional four to six petals.

- -

Hint: When making the loops with ribbon, place needle and thread on top of your work – leaving thread at the back will cause tangled knots.

- -

Flatten the petals

Use Pritt or UHU glue stick (similar to what children use for paper projects at school) and scoop some onto a tapestry or chenille needle as shown. Place needle inside loop to apply a dab of glue. Press on the loop to form a flat edge. Wipe needle with a damp cloth before starting on the next petal. Do this for every petal of the daisy.

Hint: As you press the petal's edge, lift it up off the surface of the design.

Use small, sharp embroidery scissors and cut the edges to form rounded petals. For some petals, cut a small notch into the edge for a lifelike effect.

Make the yellow and green shapes

With the blue water-soluble pen trace onto 13 mm silk ribbon no. 99: 5 x A circles. Onto 32 mm silk ribbon no. 140 trace 2 x B circles, 1 x C circle and 2 x D circles. Cut out shapes, place in a glass of water to dissolve the blue marks and lay on tissue or towel to dry. There are ten circles in total.

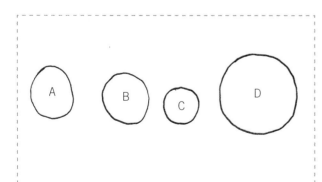

Make the yellow centres

Use the A thread with a knot at the long end. Make small running stitches around the edge of a yellow circle A; gather the thread to form a dome-like shape. Use the same needle and thread to secure the shape with tiny stab stitches, using a gentle tension so as not to flatten the shape too much.

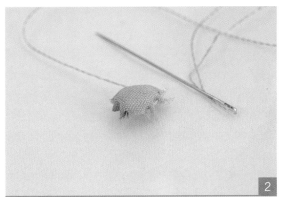

Add the shadows

With thread D, make little French knots to form a shadow along the edge of the yellow centre. Wrap thread two or three times around the needle. Refer to the picture on page 118 for the position of the shadows on this daisy and the daisies to follow.

Complete the five daisies

Use 7 mm silk ribbon no. 123 and make the blue daisies as you did the pink. Use thread B or C to secure the base of each loop. Add the yellow centres and make the brown shadows with French knots.

Do the same for the pink and blue daisies on the other side of the circle. Glue and flatten the petals and cut the ribbon to form rounded petals. Make little notches in some to form serrated petals. Add the yellow centres and shadows, as you did before.

Make the pale pink daisy

Use 7 mm ribbon no. 114 and make this daisy in ribbon stitch. Make six holes in your fabric around the pencil circle with an awl. Form the petals in ribbon stitch. See more about ribbon stitch on page 22. Use thread B and tiny stab stitches on the tip and base of each petal to secure and to re-shape if necessary.

Make the small buds

Use the no. 114 ribbon and make a padded ribbon stitch for the pink bud. Work one stitch on top of another and secure with thread B and tiny stab stitches. Repeat for the other bud with ribbon no. 115, using the same method.

- -

Hint: Work with a gentle tension, pulling needle and ribbon carefully to the back so as not to flatten the stitches.

- -

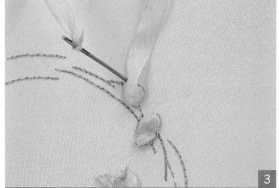

Make the green seeds and the calyx

With thread E and the smallest green circle C, make a round little seed as you did for the yellow centres. Secure alongside the pink daisy as shown. Use the B circle and repeat the process, adding it in the centre of the pink daisy to form the green calyx.

Add the last B circle a short distance away from the pink bud – refer to the pattern on page 110 and the pictures below for placement. The two D circles will be used a little later.

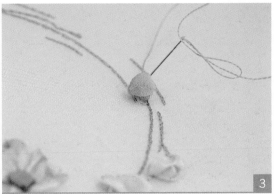

Add texture and background shadows

Use the pale blue wool fibre, pulling it apart to form a fine, soft texture. Apply around the daisies as shown. Repeat with the pale green fibre. Repeat for the entire design using a mix of blue and the

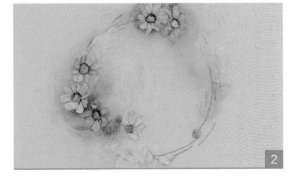

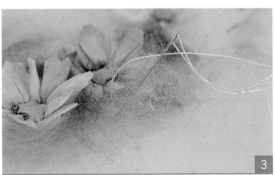

various shades of green fibre. Refer to the photographs alongside and on the previous as a guide.

Use the B thread and with tiny stab stitches, secure the fibre onto the design. Use stitches only where necessary, to hold the shape of the fibre. Gently lift some of the fibre around the stitch with the sharp point of your needle to cover the stitch if it is too visible.

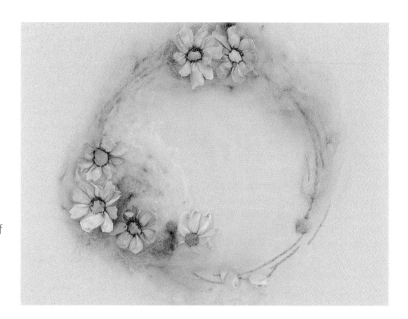

Make large seeds, stem and leaves

With thread E, make running stitches around a D circle. Form a small ball with some green fibre. Place ball on the circle and gather to form a small seed pod. Refer to the pattern on page 112 for the G circles (which are near the two daisies) and secure onto the design, as you did before.

Cut leaf shapes to your liking from the green silk paper and apply between the green seeds as shown. Use one or two straight stitches on the base of the leaves to secure. Lift the tip of the leaves for a lifelike effect. Add two more leaves under the blue daisy.

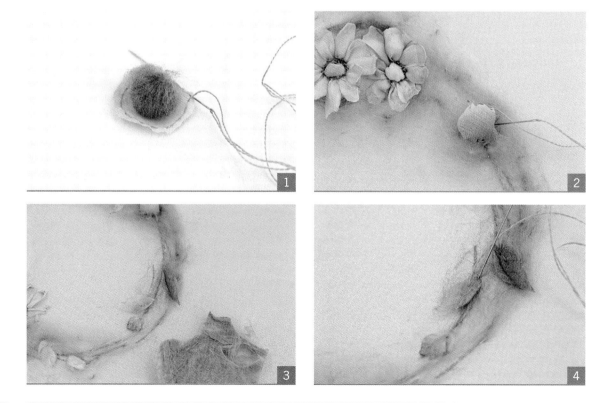

Make a stem for the pale pink daisy. From the green silk paper. Cut a thin stalk, twirl it between your fingers to form a curved stem and secure onto the design with tiny stab stitches.

Make the last green seed pod with circle D, filling it with a ball of green fibre, and secure it onto your design, as you did before.

Add more shadows

With thread E make three-wrap French knots on the calyx of the pale pink daisy. Change to thread D and add the brown shadows in the same way. Wrap thread two or three times around your needle.

Add findings

If you like, you could add little shells, flat stones or beads to create your own unique signature. Use straight stitch to secure a shell or French knots to secure a stone or bead. A little ladybird, or any quaint little charm, will work well.

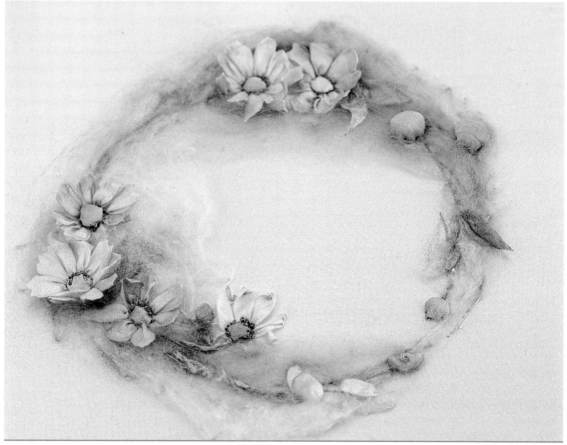

Double roses and blue violets

You will need

Ribbon

Di van Niekerk's silk and organza ribbons

	32 mm silk no. 102
	38 mm organza no. 128
	13 mm silk no. 33
	7 mm silk no. 123
	7 mm silk no. 146
	4 mm silk no. 34
	38 mm organza no. 120
	7 mm silk no. 26
	2 mm silk no. 143

Needles

- Embroidery/crewel: size 9 and 10
- Quilting/betweens: size 9 and 10
- Chenille: size 16, 18, 20 and 22
- Tapestry: size 13

What else?

Background fabric

Pale cream or off-white Dupion silk fabric, large enough to fit into a 25 cm (10 inch) hoop.

Backing fabric

White or cream organza fabric, the same size as the background above.

Thread and fibre

Separate one strand from the six and work with one strand of thread unless suggested otherwise.

DMC six-strand thread

	A. 451 mushroom
	B. 3364 medium green
	C. 159 pale blue
	D. 778 pale pink
	E. 3362 dark green

Rajmahal Art. Silk

	F. 115

Fibres

Wool fibre: dusty pink, medium grey-brown, medium blue and lilac
Silk fibre: pale green and pale blue
Silk rod: golden yellow
Silk paper: olive/sage green 10 x 5 cm (4 x 2 inch)

Fabric

- Sheer organza (synthetic): 20 cm (8 inch) square of white
- Bridal satin (synthetic): 20 cm (8 inch) square of salmon pink
- China silk (synthetic): 15 x 7.5 cm (6 x 3 inch) pale yellow

You will also need

- 25 cm (10 inch) quilting hoop
- Pins and tracing paper
- Black waterproof pigment ink pen with a fine tip
- Blue water-soluble pen
- Candle and lighter or matches
- Glass or bowl of water
- Sharp 2B pencil

Stitches used

Straight/stab stitch, split stitch, stem stitch, back stitch, split back stitch, running stitch, detached chain stitch/lazy daisy, ribbon stitch, fly stitch, French knot, twisted/twirled straight stitch and twisted/twirled ribbon stitch

Prepare the design

Trace the diagram on page 122 (stems, leaves and rose shapes) onto the background fabric with a sharp pencil. Draw neat lines and shapes for a good finish.

- -

Hint: If the fabric is a bit dark to see the design properly, use a light box or sunny window.

- -

Place organza backing fabric under the background fabric and insert both layers in the hoop. See page 10 and 11 for more about backing fabric and about inserting fabric in a hoop.

To make the roses, I used silk and organza ribbons and sumptuous silky satin fabrics. Refer to page 123 for the list of what you need.

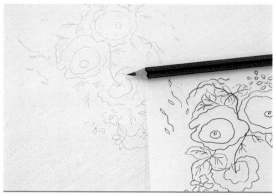

Trace and cut out the petals

Use the white organza fabric and, with a blue water-soluble pen, trace the six shapes from diagram 1. Cut out the shapes, place in a glass of water to remove the blue marks and place on a towel to dry.

- -

Hint: To prevent marks in your book, trace shapes onto a separate sheet of paper first before tracing onto organza fabric.

- -

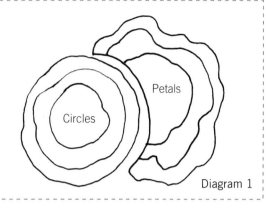

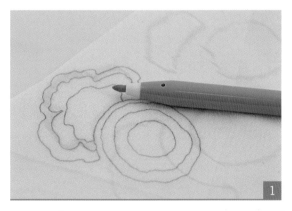

Draw four medium circles onto 32 mm silk ribbon no. 102 and another four onto 38 mm organza ribbon no. 128.

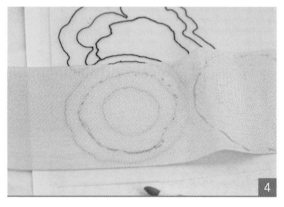

Light a candle. Use tweezers to hold the shape and singe the edge on the flame so that the shape curls up. **Caution:** Be careful not to burn yourself, and have a glass or bowl of water nearby to dip it into if it catches alight.

Draw four medium and four small petal shapes onto the same organza ribbon no. 128. Cut out the shapes. Place into glass of water to remove the blue marks. Place on a towel alongside the white shapes to dry. There are a total of 22 shapes for the first rose. Singe all the organza shapes with a flame, as you did for the white petals. **Note:** There is no need to do this with the silk shapes – they will be fine as they are. Singeing the edge of a pale coloured silk ribbon will cause brown marks. Place all shapes safely aside to use later.

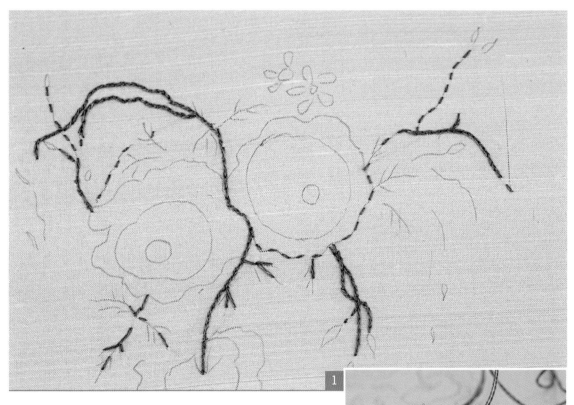

Make the stems

Use two strands of thread A and make the stems in split stitch, split back stitch or back stitch. Make short stitches, about 3 mm (⅛ inch) long, for a good finish and use an even tension throughout. As you reach the outline of the rose, make running stitches to reach the next stem. Use running stitch for some stems for an interesting effect.

With one strand of thread B, make detached chain stitches (lazy daisies) for the small green leaves. Refer to the main picture on page 121. Use the same thread and insert needle under and over each brown stitch for a thicker stem. Make the remaining stems in green thread, as you did before.

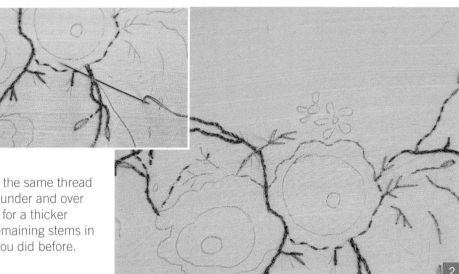

Make the leaves in ribbon stitch

Hint: Use short lengths of ribbon (15 to 20 cm or 6 to 8 inches) to prevent fraying. Thread up with silk ribbon no. 33 on a size 16 chenille needle and make the leaves in ribbon stitch. With thread A, make a stab stitch on the tip and base of each leaf to secure the stitch and then add the veins in straight stitch.

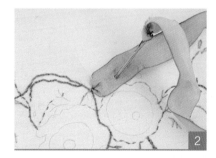

Make the violets

Hint: Use an awl or large needle to make a hole in the fabric before you make the bud to prevent the ribbon from tearing.

Use 7 mm silk ribbon no. 123 and form the petals in ribbon stitch. Make three stitches close together. Use thread C and tiny stab stitches to secure the petals at the base and tip. Repeat for the second bud. Make a French knot at the base of each bud; wrap ribbon once or twice around your needle.

Make all the petals in ribbon stitch; use thread C to secure the stitch with tiny stab stitches. Use 7 mm silk ribbon no. 146 and make the yellow centre in ribbon stitch. Make the purple stripes with thread F and straight stitch. Add a few French knots between the yellow and blue stitches, wrapping thread twice around your needle. Use thread B and straight stitch to make the green calyx of each bud.

Make the small rose

With thread D and tiny stab stitches, secure the largest white moon-shaped petal as shown. Work along the edge closest to the stem, making several stitches close together and working through all the layers as shown.

Add shapes on top of one another, working from large to small. The silk ribbon shapes should be halved as shown. Build the rose as you like – you do not need to use all the petals. I had two silk petals left over and three or four organza petals. Everyone will have a different rose, so choose what suits your taste. Use the D thread and tiny stab stitches to secure the petals along the stem as shown. Tear a small piece of lilac wool fibre; insert it under the bottom petal to add texture. This will help lift the petals and add a shadow at the same time. Use your scissors or needle to push the fibre under the petal and secure along the stem with small stitches.

- -

Hint: Use pins to hold all petals in place until you have stitched them onto the design.

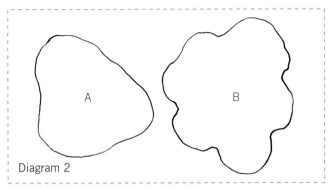

Diagram 2

Trace two A shapes onto the salmon pink satin and prepare as you did the organza. Stitch two petals on top of the others, as shown. Trace one B petal onto mostly yellow part of organza ribbon no. 128 and prepare as you did the others. Place between the rose petals to add more yellow and secure as shown.

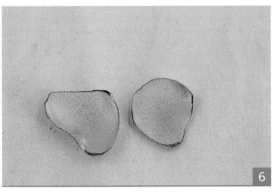
6

7

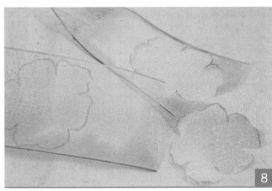
8

9

Make the twirled stems

Use 4 mm silk ribbon no. 34 and make the rose stem in twisted/twirled straight stitch. Allow needle to hang off the back of your work so that the ribbon unwinds itself. Come up to form the green calyx. Make a French knot as shown, wrapping ribbon twice around the needle.

1

2

Form the green sepals of the calyx in ribbon stitch – make two loose/puffed ribbon stitches.

- -

Hint: If you find that your tension is a bit tight and you are pulling the stitches too flat, work over a spare tapestry needle.

- -

Place a small piece of lilac fibre under the satin petals for a plump, rounded effect; make another two ribbon stitches with the green ribbon, securing the fibre at the same time.

Make two more twirled stems for the leaves. Use twisted straight or twisted ribbon stitch. Thread up with one strand of thread A and secure the stems with tiny stab stitches using a gentle tension, stitching through the ribbon so that the stitch is almost invisible. Place stitches only where necessary – where you would like the stem to curve or where you feel the stem is too loose on the design.

Create shadows and texture

Use the same thread and make straight stitches or French knots between the green sepals to create shadows. Tear off a small piece of green fibre; tease it out to form a thin layer. Place on top of the stem and the small leaves as shown in the picture. This will form a lovely feathery texture. Use the pink, grey-brown, pale blue and green fibre – add these alongside the rose and leaves as shown. Use the C thread and tiny stab stitches (placed only where necessary) to gently hold the fibre in place. The fibre is naturally clingy and will stay in place unless deliberately disturbed.

Pink leaves

Green leaves

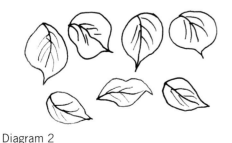

Diagram 2

Trace the teardrop shapes onto a pink part of the organza ribbon no. 120. Cut and prepare the organza petals as you did before. Add pink leaves, securing with thread B. Use tiny straight stitches on the base of each leaf. Add three to five leaves, as desired. Refer to the main picture on page 121.

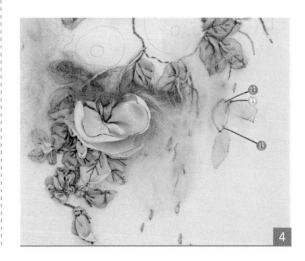

Add texture by using green silk paper. Cut out leaf shapes similar in size and shape to the leaves in the diagram 2. With thread E, secure silk leaves onto your design as shown. Silk paper sometimes allows you to separate the layers to create very thin leaves. These are useful for adding a shadow of a leaf on the outer edges of the design. Here I used thin leaves on the right-hand side of the rose, between the rose and the pink leaves.

Hint: Once the roses are completed, you will add more leaves in the same way.

Make the large roses

Make the yellow stamens with a 2 cm (¾ inch) piece of the yellow silk rod. At the one end, cut small notches into the silk rod: 1 cm (⅜ inch) long and 2 mm (¹⁄₁₆ inch) wide.

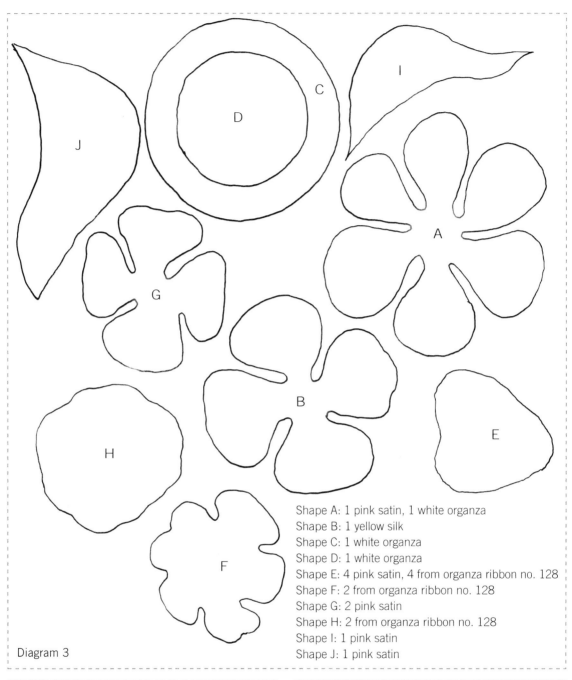

Shape A: 1 pink satin, 1 white organza
Shape B: 1 yellow silk
Shape C: 1 white organza
Shape D: 1 white organza
Shape E: 4 pink satin, 4 from organza ribbon no. 128
Shape F: 2 from organza ribbon no. 128
Shape G: 2 pink satin
Shape H: 2 from organza ribbon no. 128
Shape I: 1 pink satin
Shape J: 1 pink satin

Diagram 3

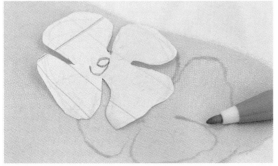

Trace the shapes onto the fabric and ribbon with the blue water-soluble pen – refer to the list with diagram 3 to see how many shapes you need for one large rose. Cut out the shapes and place in a glass of water to remove the marks. Place on a towel to dry. Singe the edges of the organza shapes as you did before. Place the shapes alongside the labelled paper shapes to serve as a useful guide.

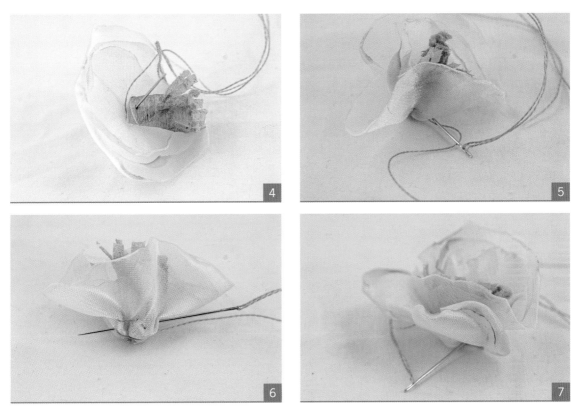

Use the B thread with a knot at the long end. Place shapes C, H and D on top of one another, large to small. Place yellow stamen on top. Secure with stab stitches, twirling fabric around the yellow stamen to make the centre of the rose. Use several stitches, inserting the needle into all the layers as shown. Take yellow shape B, fold it in half and secure onto the rose with same thread and stitches, inserting the needle through all the layers several times.

Take a G shape and place it on the rose, right side facing outwards. Secure with green thread. Use the second G shape and repeat as shown.

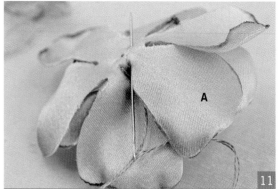

Place rose on top of the pink A shape. Secure as you did before, stitching through all the layers. Place white A shape onto your design as shown, secure with D thread; use three or four stitches in the centre of the shape. Stitch the rose onto the white shape, working through some of the layers to secure. Use a gentle tension so as not to flatten the rose and note how the rose is facing slightly down and outward. See the main picture on page 137.

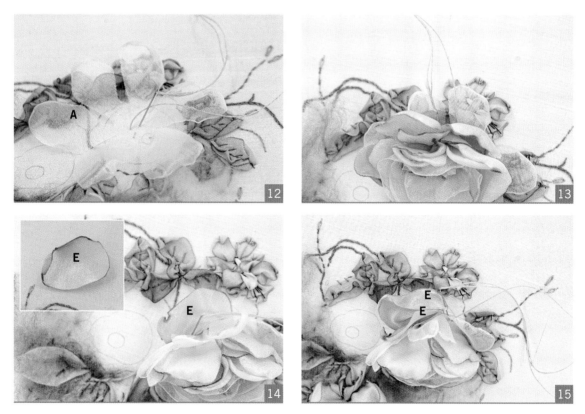

Take a pink E shape and make the outer petal. Place petal with satin side facing the rose. Stitch onto your design with pink thread D and tiny stab stitches, working close to the rose for an authentic effect. Repeat with a second E shape as shown. See how the satin side is still facing the rose?

Use the F and H organza shapes and insert between the rose and the background fabric to create the outer petals. Repeat until you are happy with the rose, pinning the shapes in place and securing with the pink thread as you did before. Add more petals between the others until you are happy with your rose. Use small, sharp embroidery scissors to trim some petals if necessary. You could also trim the stamens slightly if they are too prominent for your liking.

Take petal I and place it (satin side facing out) to form a dome-like shape over the rose petals. Secure in place with D thread. Work with a gentle tension so as not to flatten the rose. Use petal J and, with satin side facing up, stitch it onto the fabric to form the large outer petal.

Add more leaves

Use the silk paper and cut out leaf shapes as you did before. Tear off thin layers and add more leaves on the right-hand side and under the rose to complete this section.

Make the third rose

Repeat the process: make the third rose in the same way as the second. I used fewer petals for this rose – it is smaller than the others.

Hint: To re-shape the petals, use a large tapestry needle: insert between the petals to re-shape them to your liking.

Optional: If you prefer darker green leaves and sepals, use 7 mm silk ribbon no. 26 and add dark green detail in ribbon stitch.
I have accentuated the top left corner on the left-hand side of the design, see page 124. Use thread E and make a knot at the long end. With 2 mm ribbon no. 143, make one long straight stitch, working from bottom left to the top left corner. Pull ribbon taut and come up to form the top line in the same way. Pull ribbon taut again to form a straight line. Use thread to secure ribbon at the back with tiny stitches, holding ribbon taut until it is secure. Use the same thread and running stitch to stitch the ribbon onto the design. The stitches and the gaps between them are roughly 4 mm (a bit over $\frac{1}{8}$ inch) long.

Wild roses and pink blossoms

You will need

Ribbon

Di van Niekerk's silk and organza ribbons

 7 mm silk no. 19
7 mm silk no. 140
32 mm silk no. 114
7 mm silk no. 16

Needles

- Embroidery/crewel: size 5 to 10 (mixed pack)
- Chenille: size 18 to 24 (mixed pack)
- Quilting/betweens: size 10
- Tapestry: size 13

What else?

Background fabric

Off-white to pale cream silk-satin or bridal satin, large enough to fit into a 25 cm (10 inch) hoop.

Backing fabric

A pale colour organza, same size as above.

Thread and fibre

Separate one strand from the six and work with one strand of thread unless suggested otherwise.

DvN Perlé 12

 A. 131 brown

DMC six-strand thread

B. 3364 green
C. 729 mustard
D. 3832 dark pink
E. 819 pale pink

Fabric, fibres and yarn

- Organza fabric: sheer (synthetic) organza, white 10 x 20 cm (4 x 8 inch)
- Wool fibre: medium pink, darker pink, medium yellow, pale salmon, medium brown
- Silk fibre: medium to pale green, pale blue
- Silk paper: olive to sage green 10 x 5 cm (4 x 2 inch): pale slate grey 2.5 x 2.5 cm (1 x 1 inch)
- Silk rods: salmon to pale pink – two rods, approximately 12.5 x 3 cm (5 x 1.2 inch)

You will also need

- Tracing paper and sharp 2B pencil
- 25 cm (10 inch) quilting hoop and pins
- Candle and lighter or matches
- Optional: anti-fray agent, clear water-soluble liquid

Stitches used

Couching and whipped couching, straight/stab stitch, ribbon stitch, French knot, pistil stitch (extended French knot), twisted/twirled straight stitch, twisted/twirled ribbon stitch

Prepare the design

For this project I used a silk-satin background in the softest shade of cream. Dupion silk or pure linen in off-white or natural would also be a good choice. For the backing fabric, use soft grey, white or cream organza fabric. Both blocks of fabric are the same size: large enough to fit in a 25 cm or 10 inch hoop. Use a sharp 2B pencil and neatly trace diagram B onto your background.

Hint: Keep lines as thin as possible so they won't show through once embroidered. Place the fabric in your hoop as shown on page 11.

Diagram B

Make stems, branches, leaves and calyxes

Use the A thread; couch a stem into place using the same thread on a second needle. Space couching stitches about 5 mm ($\frac{3}{16}$ inch) apart. Refer to diagram B as a guide. Work over the leaves and circles – these will be made on top a little later.

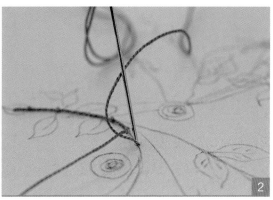

Hint: The formation of the stems and branches is essential – this is the framework onto which you will be building your design. To form a neat couching stitch, move the laid thread a little to the side to see where to insert needle back into the same hole. This way the couching stitch is not too wide and untidy. Move laid thread back into place to form the next stitch. For tiny leaf stalks leading off the stem, use small straight/stab stitches. If you would like to form a thicker stem, whip the couched stem with the same thread: see whipped couching in the Stitch gallery on page 157.

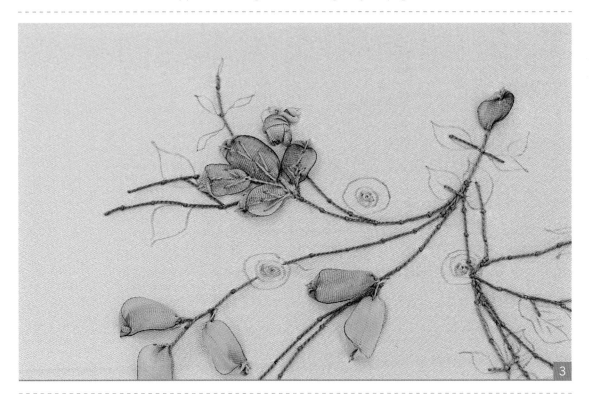

Hint: For easy placement of the leaves, make a yellow French knot in the space where the roses will be. Refer to the circles of each rose in diagram C on page 144. Use two strands of thread C and wind thread twice around your needle. The yellow dots will serve as a good guide.

With short lengths of 7 mm ribbon no. 19 and 140, make the leaves in ribbon stitch. See diagram C below for placement guide. Use thread B and tiny stab stitches at the base and tip of every leaf to secure the stitch. With the same thread, secure the ribbon tails at the back. Come up to form veins on some leaves in straight stitch.

Note: It is not necessary to make veins on all the leaves. For wider leaves, make two ribbon stitches alongside and overlapping each other.

Diagram C

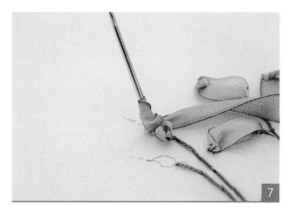

Form round calyxes with a French knot, wrapping ribbon twice around your needle. To form a smooth surface, cover the knot with a ribbon stitch as shown. Use B thread and make tiny stab stitches to secure the stitch and to reshape it if necessary.

For the longer green buds, make two ribbon stitches alongside each other.

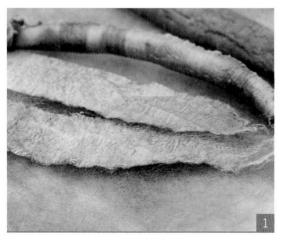

Make the wild roses and blossoms

The base of each rose is made by cutting shapes out of salmon pink silk rods which have been ironed flat. You could use another colour instead, like golden yellow or a rich red, for example.

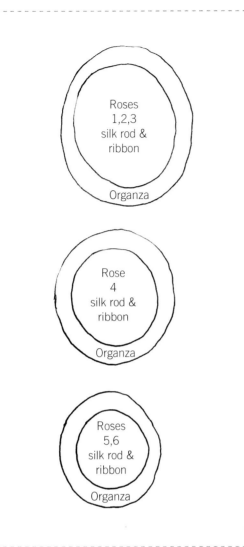

Refer to diagram C on page 144 for the numbered roses – the circles (left) are numbered accordingly. Trace the small (inner) circles onto tracing paper and cut out the paper shapes. Place on top of the silk rod and cut out six circles – one for each rose. Crumple up the silk circle to form a cup-like shape.

Roses 1,2,3 silk rod & ribbon
Organza

Rose 4 silk rod & ribbon
Organza

Roses 5,6 silk rod & ribbon
Organza

Secure onto your design with thread D. Use one or two stab stitches in the centre, stitching through all the layers. Repeat for all six roses.

Hint: If you find the shape is a little flat, make a stitch, and as you insert the needle into the shape, pierce and move the shape with your needle to form a fold. Then take needle to the back of your work.

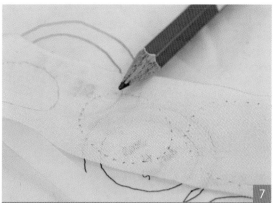

Make another six shapes (two of each size) from the inner circles on page 146. With the 2B pencil and a dotted line as shown, trace the shapes onto the 32 mm silk ribbon no. 114. Secure a circle on top of the rose with the D thread and stab stitch.

Scrunch it up: as you insert the needle into the circle, pierce it, forming a fold before taking needle to the back of your work. Repeat for all six roses.

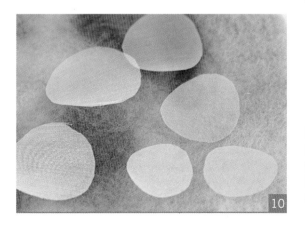

Form the outer circles on page 146 and with a 2B pencil, draw six shapes (two of each size) onto the white organza fabric. Cut out inside the pencil line – the pencil marks should not be visible along the edge if possible.

Light a candle. Use tweezers to hold the shape and singe the edge on the flame so that the shape curls up. **Caution:** Be careful not to burn yourself, and have a bowl of water nearby to dip it into if it catches alight.

Place an organza shape on top of the rose and secure with thread C, as you did before.

Repeat for all six roses.

Fold roses 4 and 5 by using a few tiny stab stitches to hold the shape.

Form yellow stamens inside the roses with French knots. Use thread C and wrap thread three times around your needle.

Add the pink shadows inside the rose with thread D – make three or four French knots close to the yellow ones.

Tear small pieces of wool and silk fibre (pink, salmon, green and yellow) and twirl each colour between your fingertips to make thin strips.

Form circular shapes with the fibre and place inside the rose. Use tiny stab stitches to secure fibres around the stamens. Place stitches only where necessary to hold fibres in place and use a gentle tension so as not to flatten the fibre too much. Use the same D thread and straight stitch to add pink shadows on the tips of some leaves; make small thorns leading from the stems and add pink veins on some leaves. See the enlarged picture on page 151.

Make the calyxes and twirled stems

With 7 mm ribbon no. 16, make the calyxes of roses 5 and 4. Make a French knot and cover it with a ribbon stitch for a smooth finish. Make the sepals in ribbon stitch.

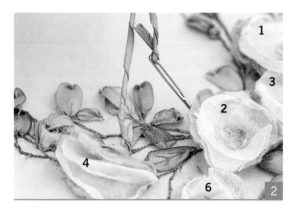

With the same colour, make the stems with twisted/twirled straight stitch. Twirl the ribbon to form a tight coil before taking the needle to the back. Use a gentle tension and allow the ribbon to unwind at the back before coming up to form the next stem. This will prevent loops from forming at the back of your work.

Hint: Thread the needle under some leaves (if you like) before inserting it into the fabric to form the stitch. Make twirled stems leading from the small buds and leading up to and off rose 3. Refer to the enlarged picture on page 151 for more detail.

Use thread B and tiny stab stitches to secure loose parts of the twisted stem. These stitches are only necessary where the stem is a bit loose and where it needs to have more of a curve. Work between the twirls so that the stitches are almost invisible. Make the little pink bud by pushing a tiny piece of pink fibre under the ribbon stitches, and use the D thread to secure along the side. At the same time make long straight stitches on the tips of the buds.

The final details

This is an optional and wonderful way to add a feathery texture (and colour) to your design. Use wisps of wool and silky fibre to form shadows and background texture. It is a good idea to create shadows under the roses for dimension. Tear bits of brown fibre and place them under the roses. Use your scissors to gently push the fibre underneath. Tear a piece of grey silk paper and place under rose 5 as shown. Next, tear thin pieces of pale green and yellow, then add the palest blue on the outer edges. See the picture below. Place everything as you would like it to (refer to the opposite page for making and placing of the silk paper leaves.

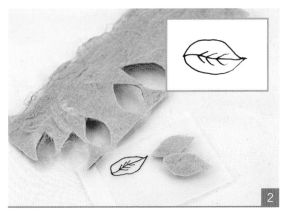

Use the green silk paper and refer to the leaf shape on this page as a guide. Cut approximately 10 leaves similar in size.

Place amongst the roses, on top of the fibre, and use thread E to secure the shapes with small stab stitches.

Use the same stitch and secure other fibres onto your fabric. Space stitches only where necessary to hold the fibres in place.

Work with a gentle tension so as not to pull the adjoining pieces out of place, holding the thread so that it does not catch onto the fibres and leaves.

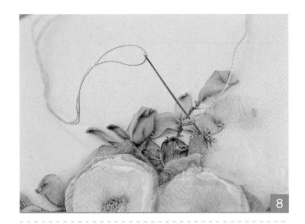

With the D thread, make pink veins on the leaves in straight stitch, allowing the tip of the leaves to be lifted off your design. Add more fibre where you see fit. See how I added grey fibre under rose 1 for balance ?

Add a few more golden yellow stamens with thread C and use French knots (three wraps around needle). Refer to the picture and add more detail until you are happy with your creation.

Hint: If you like, you could make another (slightly bigger) organza shape and place it on top of rose 3 to create a larger rose.

Stitches

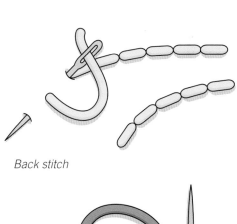

Back stitch

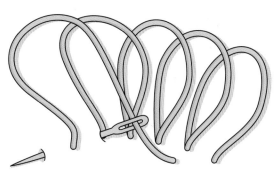

Back stitch, looped

Back stitch, whipped

Chain stitch

Chain stitch, whipped

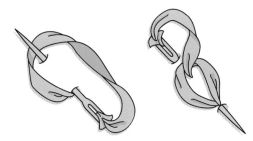

Chain, detached/Lazy daisy

Couching

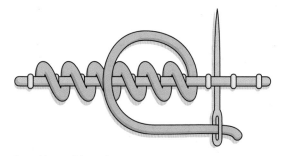

Couching, whipped

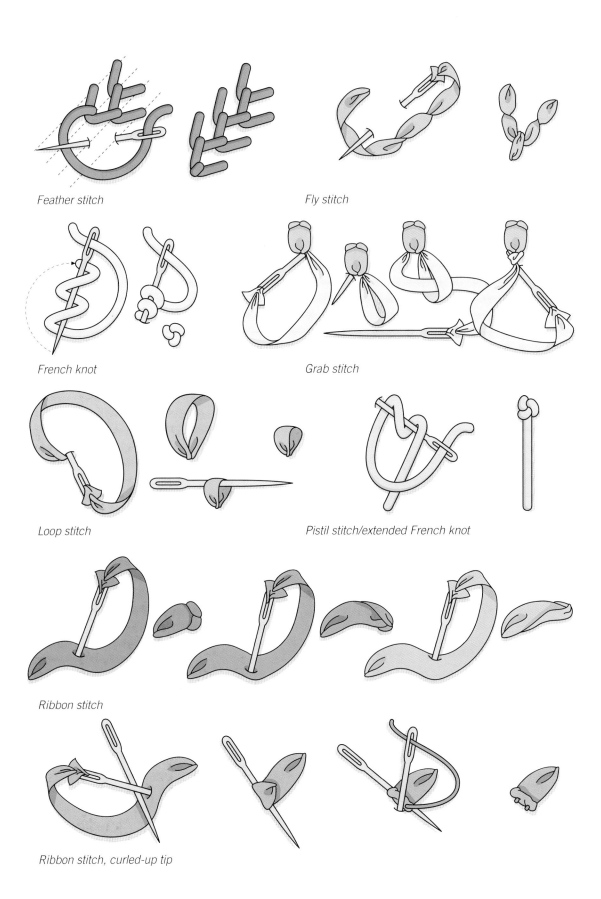

Feather stitch

Fly stitch

French knot

Grab stitch

Loop stitch

Pistil stitch/extended French knot

Ribbon stitch

Ribbon stitch, curled-up tip

Ribbon stitch, double

Ribbon stitch, loose/puffed (worked over needle)   *Ribbon stitch, padded*

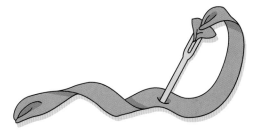

Ribbon stitch, twisted/twirled

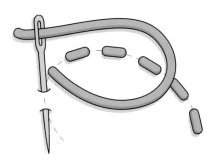

Running stitch   *Split back stitch*

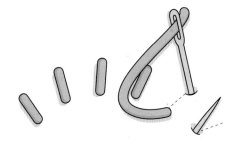

Split stitch   *Stab stitch*

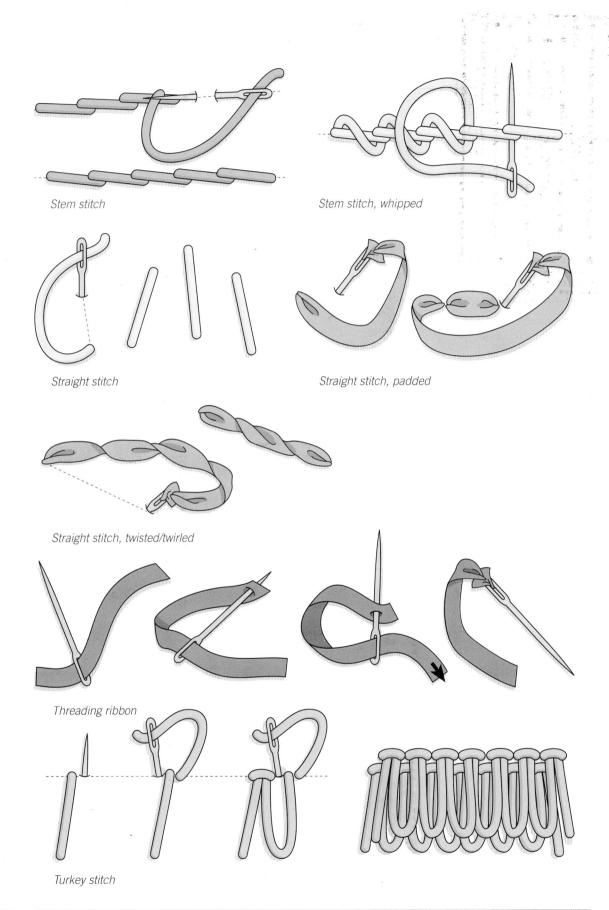

Stem stitch

Stem stitch, whipped

Straight stitch

Straight stitch, padded

Straight stitch, twisted/twirled

Threading ribbon

Turkey stitch